Quick & Tasty Vegetarian

Contents

Introduction

Fruit and vegetables, which are natural sources of vitamins and minerals, form the basis of a huge variety of meals. These foods offer a multitude of different colours and variety of tastes which, when combined with herbs and spices, create an explosion of sumptuous flavours. Due to the enormous variety of foods available on the vegetarian menu, vegetarian cooking is now extremely popular with meat-eaters, vegetarians and vegans alike. Tasty Vegetarian has combined the most traditional vegetarian dishes with new recipes which together offer some unique and exciting flavours and textures. From pâtés or bhajis as starters, stuffed vegetables and pasta as main courses, to delicious chocolate fudge pudding or butterscotch melts for desserts, this collection of recipes covers all areas of vegetarian cuisine.

Tasty Vegetarian Food

Vegetarian food has come a long way since the nut cutlet! Its growing popularity is due, at least in part, to the diverse range of influences – from Asia and North Africa, to Italy and Mexico – which have introduced to us a whole new range of exciting ingredients enabling us to make delicious recipes from around the world.

A wide variety of exotic foods can now easily be obtained in local supermarkets. These offer novel textures and flavours making vegetarian cooking more interesting than ever. Try Kashmiri Spinach or a Middle Eastern Salad or why not enjoy a delicious Spanish Tortilla accompanied by Sidekick Vegetables.

Healthy Eating

Many people turn to vegetarian food because it is so healthy. Fruit and vegetables are naturally fat-free and provide plenty of fibre, carbohydrates, vitamins and minerals. Each particular food has a different nutritional benefit and this should be kept in mind when combining various ingredients to ensure a balanced diet.

In varying degrees, fruit and vegetables contain calcium, iron and phosphorous, all of which are important for healthy living. Furthermore, fruit and vegetables are great sources of vitamins. Vitamin A is found in green, yellow and orange vegetables, and particularly in carrots. Leafy vegetables are an excellent source of vitamin E. Vitamin C is present in many 'fruit vegetables', such as peppers and tomatoes, and may also be found in the roots and leaves of others. Vegetarians should ensure that sufficient levels of protein are maintained in their diets. This is not difficult however, as vegetables can be eaten with pulses or legumes which offer natural sources of protein.

Pulses

Pulses are extremely important to a vegetarian diet and can be found in many forms; from lentils and haricot (navy) beans, to kidney beans and split peas. The nutritional benefits of legumes include high levels of carbohydrates, vitamins – especially vitamin B – and notably iron, which is especially important for women and the elderly. Each of the different pulses gives a different texture to your dish and all can be combined with a rich variety of flavours.

World wide, local gastronomies have influenced the methods of preparing, cooking and serving different

legumes enormously. From Massachusetts, the home of the baked bean, to Mexico, and the ubiquitous frijoles or refried beans, to the tasty lentil dhal of India, each region has found an innovative way of spicing up their food.

Eating meals which combine pulses with grains ensures you achieve the complete daily protein required in a healthy diet, so, for example, it is an excellent idea to mop up a lentil soup with tasty wholewheat bread. Recipes have been included in Tasty Vegetarian which show you how to combine different food groups to create a variety of flavoursome dishes. Choose from Deep South Rice & Beans, Spiced Rice & Lentils or Moroccan Salad, among others, for a completely balanced meal.

Choosing and Cooking Vegetables

With such a huge variety of vegetables on the market, it is important to choose and cook them in the correct way. When purchasing vegetables make sure that they are neither damaged nor bruised. Leafy vegetables should look green, not yellow, and the leaves should not be slimy or wilting. Root vegetables should be firm with a dull and dry appearance. Fruit should have taut, shiny skins and be firm to the touch.

Preparing vegetables incorrectly can lead to a leaching of vitamins and loss of all-important nutrients. Many vegetables can be eaten raw but cooking often enhances the flavour and changes their texture. There are many different ways they can be prepared, some of which do not require fat. Grilling and barbecuing leaves the food with a crisp outer coating whilst maintaining moist and tender interiors; braising and stewing involve cooking the dish very slowly using liquids – often the natural juices of the ingredients – resulting in tender vegetables which retain all their nutrients, flavours and aromas; boiling and poaching do not use any fat but can lead to loss of essential food groups to the cooking water which is discarded.

If you do boil your vegetables, try to keep cooking times as short as possible to limit the extraction of essential vitamins. And remember, the cooking water can be used afterwards to make soups and sauces as it will be full of flavour and nutrients. Steaming is a healthier alternative to boiling as less water comes into contact with the food. Instead of conventional frying, try stir-frying in a wok as this requires minimal fat and helps retain the goodness and colour of the ingredients.

Cooking Vegetarian for the First Time

For those who have decided to convert to vegetarianism and are cooking meat-free food for the first time there are several ingredients that should be avoided. In particular, gelatine, a protein used to thicken foods, is used in many puddings, however it is made from collagen so a vegetarian substitute should be used instead. Also, many cheeses are made with animal derivatives: strict vegetarians should buy those that have been certified by the Vegetarian Society and have a green 'V' on the label. Vegetarian cheeses are made with rennets of non-animal origin, using microbial or fungal enzymes. When buying pre-packaged ingredients, in particular sweet foods such as biscuits, always check the ingredients to see if animal fats have been used. You should also be aware that some condiments, such as Worcestershire Sauce which is made using anchovies, may contain animal products.

KEY

- Simplicity level 1 - 3 (1 easiest, 3 slightly harder)
- Preparation time
- Cooking time

Vegetable & Corn Chowder

This is a really filling soup, which should be served before a light main course. It is easy to prepare and filled with flavour.

NUTRITIONAL INFORMATION

Calories	378	Sugars	20g
Protein	16g	Fat	13g
Carbohydrate	52g	Saturates	6g

15 MINS 30 MINS

SERVES 4

INGREDIENTS

1 tbsp vegetable oil

1 red onion, diced

1 red (bell) pepper, seeded and diced

3 garlic cloves, crushed

1 large potato, diced

2 tbsp plain (all-purpose) flour

600 ml/1 pint/2½ cups milk

300 ml/½ pint/1¼ cups vegetable stock

50 g/1¾ oz broccoli florets

300 g/10½ oz/3 cups canned sweetcorn (corn), drained

75 g/2¾ oz/¾ cup Cheddar cheese, grated

salt and pepper

1 tbsp chopped coriander (cilantro), to garnish

1

2

4

1 Heat the oil in a large saucepan. Add the onion, (bell) pepper, garlic and potato and sauté over a low heat, stirring frequently, for 2–3 minutes.

2 Stir in the flour and cook, stirring for 30 seconds. Gradually stir in the milk and stock.

3 Add the broccoli and sweetcorn (corn). Bring the mixture to the boil, stirring constantly, then reduce the heat and simmer for about 20 minutes, or until all the vegetables are tender.

4 Stir in 50 g/1¾ oz/½ cup of the cheese until it melts.

5 Season and spoon the chowder into a warm soup tureen. Garnish with the remaining cheese and the coriander (cilantro) and serve.

COOK'S TIP

Vegetarian cheeses are made with rennets of non-animal origin, using microbial or fungal enzymes.

Pumpkin Soup

This is an American classic that has now become popular worldwide. When pumpkin is out of season use butternut squash in its place.

NUTRITIONAL INFORMATION	
Calories 112	Sugars 7g
Protein 4g	Fat 7g
Carbohydrate 8g	Saturates 2g

10 MINS

30 MINS

SERVES 6

INGREDIENTS

- about 1 kg/2 lb 4 oz pumpkin
- 40 g/1½ oz/3 tbsp butter or margarine
- 1 onion, sliced thinly
- 1 garlic clove, crushed
- 900 ml/1½ pints/3½ cups vegetable stock
- ½ tsp ground ginger
- 1 tbsp lemon juice
- 3–4 thinly pared strips of orange rind (optional)
- 1–2 bay leaves or 1 bouquet garni
- 300 ml/½ pint/1¼ cups milk
- salt and pepper

TO GARNISH

- 4–6 tablespoons single (light) or double (heavy) cream, natural yogurt or fromage frais
- snipped chives

1

5

6

1 Peel the pumpkin, remove the seeds and then cut the flesh into 2.5 cm/1 inch cubes.

2 Melt the butter or margarine in a large, heavy-based saucepan. Add the onion and garlic and fry over a low heat until soft but not coloured.

3 Add the pumpkin and toss with the onion for 2–3 minutes.

4 Add the stock and bring to the boil over a medium heat. Season to taste with salt and pepper and add the ginger, lemon juice, strips of orange rind, if using, and bay leaves or bouquet garni. Cover and simmer over a low heat for about 20 minutes, until the pumpkin is tender.

5 Discard the orange rind, if using, and the bay leaves or bouquet garni. Cool the soup slightly, then press through a strainer or process in a food processor until smooth. Pour into a clean saucepan.

6 Add the milk and reheat gently. Adjust the seasoning. Garnish with a swirl of cream, natural yogurt or fromage frais and snipped chives, and serve.

Spanish Tortilla

This classic Spanish dish is often served as part of a tapas (appetizer) selection. A variety of cooked vegetables can be added to this recipe.

NUTRITIONAL INFORMATION			
Calories	430	Sugars	6g
Protein	16g	Fat	20g
Carbohydrate	50g	Saturates	4g

10 MINS 35 MINS

SERVES 4

INGREDIENTS

- 1 kg/2 lb 4 oz waxy potatoes, thinly sliced
- 4 tbsp vegetable oil
- 1 onion, sliced
- 2 garlic cloves, crushed
- 1 green (bell) pepper, seeded and diced
- 2 tomatoes, seeded and chopped
- 25 g/1 oz canned sweetcorn (corn), drained
- 6 large eggs, beaten
- 2 tbsp chopped parsley
- salt and pepper

1 Parboil the potatoes in a saucepan of lightly salted boiling water for 5 minutes. Drain well.

2 Heat the oil in a large frying pan (skillet), add the potato and onions and sauté over a low heat, stirring constantly, for 5 minutes, until the potatoes have browned.

3 Add the garlic, diced (bell) pepper, chopped tomatoes and sweetcorn (corn), mixing well.

4 Pour in the eggs and add the chopped parsley. Season well with salt and pepper. Cook for 10-12 minutes, until the underside is cooked through.

5 Remove the frying pan (skillet) from the heat and continue to cook the tortilla under a preheated medium grill (broiler) for 5-7 minutes, or until the tortilla is set and the top is golden brown.

6 Cut the tortilla into wedges or cubes, depending on your preference, and transfer to serving dishes. Serve with salad. In Spain tortillas are served hot, cold or warm.

COOK'S TIP

Ensure that the handle of your pan is heatproof before placing it under the grill (broiler) and be sure to use an oven glove when removing it as it will be very hot.

Vegetable Medley

This is a colourful dish of shredded vegetables in a fresh garlic and honey dressing. It is delicious served with crusty bread.

NUTRITIONAL INFORMATION			
Calories	209	Sugars	10g
Protein	2g	Fat	14g
Carbohydrate	20g	Saturates	2g

15 MINS   5 MINS

SERVES 4

INGREDIENTS

- 2 tbsp olive oil
- 1 potato, cut into thin strips
- 1 fennel bulb, cut into thin strips
- 2 carrots, grated
- 1 red onion, cut into thin strips
- chopped chives and fennel fronds, to garnish

DRESSING

- 3 tbsp olive oil
- 1 tbsp garlic wine vinegar
- 1 garlic clove, crushed
- 1 tsp Dijon mustard
- 2 tsp clear honey
- salt and pepper

1 Heat the olive oil in a frying pan (skillet), add the potato and fennel slices and cook over a medium heat for about 2–3 minutes, until beginning to brown. Remove from the frying pan (skillet) with a slotted spoon and drain on kitchen paper (paper towels).

2 Arrange the carrot, red onion, potato and fennel in separate piles on a serving platter.

3 Mix the dressing ingredients together and pour over the vegetables. Toss well and sprinkle with chopped chives and fennel fronds. Serve immediately or leave in the refrigerator until required.

VARIATION

Use mixed, grilled (bell) peppers or shredded leeks in this dish for variety, or add bean sprouts and a segmented orange, if you prefer.

Vegetable Fritters

These mixed vegetable fritters are coated in a light batter and deep-fried until golden. They are ideal with the sweet and sour dipping sauce.

NUTRITIONAL INFORMATION			
Calories	479	Sugars	18g
Protein	8g	Fat	32g
Carbohydrate	42g	Saturates	5g

20 MINS — 20 MINS

SERVES 4

INGREDIENTS

- 100 g/3½ oz/¾ cup wholemeal (whole wheat) flour
- pinch of cayenne pepper
- 4 tsp olive oil
- 12 tbsp cold water
- 100 g/3½ oz broccoli florets
- 100 g/3½ oz cauliflower florets
- 50 g/1¾ oz mangetout (snow peas)
- 1 large carrot, cut into batons
- 1 red (bell) pepper, seeded and sliced
- 2 egg whites, beaten
- oil, for deep-frying
- salt

SAUCE

- 150 ml/¼ pint/⅔ cup pineapple juice
- 150 ml/¼ pint/⅔ cup vegetable stock
- 2 tbsp white wine vinegar
- 2 tbsp light brown sugar
- 2 tsp cornflour (cornstarch)
- 2 spring onions (scallions), chopped

1

4

4

1 Sift the flour and a pinch of salt into a mixing bowl and add the cayenne pepper. Make a well in the centre and gradually beat in the oil and cold water to make a smooth batter.

2 Cook the vegetables in boiling water for 5 minutes and drain well.

3 Whisk the egg whites until they form peaks and gently fold them into the flour batter.

4 Dip the vegetables into the batter, turning to coat well. Drain off any excess batter. Heat the oil for deep-frying in a deep-fryer to 180°C/350°F or until a cube of bread browns in 30 seconds. Fry the coated vegetables, in batches, for 1–2 minutes, until golden. Remove from the oil with a slotted spoon and drain on kitchen paper (paper towels).

5 Place all of the sauce ingredients in a pan and bring to the boil, stirring, until thickened and clear. Serve with the fritters.

Hummus & Garlic Toasts

Hummus is a real favourite spread on these flavoursome garlic toasts for a delicious starter or snack.

NUTRITIONAL INFORMATION	
Calories 731	Sugars 2g
Protein 22g	Fat 55g
Carbohydrate ...39g	Saturates 8g

20 MINS 3 MINS

SERVES 4

INGREDIENTS

HUMMUS

- 400 g/14 oz can chickpeas (garbanzo beans)
- juice of 1 large lemon
- 6 tbsp tahini (sesame seed paste)
- 2 tbsp olive oil
- 2 garlic cloves, crushed
- salt and pepper
- chopped coriander (cilantro) and black olives, to garnish

TOASTS

- 1 ciabatta loaf (Italian bread), sliced
- 2 garlic cloves, crushed
- 1 tbsp chopped coriander (cilantro)
- 4 tbsp olive oil

2

3

5

1 To make the hummus, firstly drain the chickpeas (garbanzo beans), reserving a little of the liquid. Put the chickpeas (garbanzo beans) and liquid in a food processor and process, gradually adding the reserved liquid and lemon juice. Blend well after each addition until smooth.

2 Stir in the tahini (sesame seed paste) and all but 1 teaspoon of the olive oil. Add the garlic, season to taste and blend again until smooth.

3 Spoon the hummus into a serving dish and smooth the top. Drizzle the remaining olive oil over the top, garnish with chopped coriander (cilantro) and olives. Set aside in the refrigerator to chill while you are preparing the toasts.

4 Place the slices of ciabatta (Italian bread) on a grill (broiler) rack in a single layer.

5 Mix the garlic, coriander (cilantro) and olive oil together and drizzle over the bread slices. Cook under a hot grill (broiler), turning once, for about 2–3 minutes, until golden brown. Serve the toasts immediately with the hummus.

COOK'S TIP

Make the hummus 1 day in advance, and chill, covered, in the refrigerator until required. Garnish and serve.

Garlicky Mushroom Pakoras

Whole mushrooms are dunked in a spiced garlicky batter and deep-fried until golden. They are at their most delicious served piping hot.

NUTRITIONAL INFORMATION			
Calories	297	Sugars	3g
Protein	5g	Fat	21g
Carbohydrate	24g	Saturates	2g

20 MINS — 10-15 MINS

SERVES 6

INGREDIENTS

- 175 g/6 oz/1½ cups gram flour
- ½ tsp salt
- ¼ tsp baking powder
- 1 tsp cumin seeds
- ½-1 tsp chilli powder
- 200 ml/7 fl oz/scant 1cup water
- 2 garlic cloves, crushed
- 1 small onion, finely chopped
- vegetable oil, for deep-frying
- 500 g/1 lb 2 oz button mushrooms, trimmed and wiped
- lemon wedges and coriander (cilantro) sprigs, to garnish

1 Put the gram flour, salt, baking powder, cumin and chilli powder into a bowl and mix well together. Make a well in the centre of the mixture and gradually stir in the water, mixing thoroughly to form a batter.

2 Stir the crushed garlic and the chopped onion into the batter and leave the mixture to infuse for 10 minutes. One-third fill a deep-fat fryer or pan with vegetable oil and heat to 180°C/350°F or until a cube of bread browns in 30 seconds. Lower the basket into the hot oil.

3 Meanwhile, mix the mushrooms into the batter, stirring to coat. Remove a few at a time and place them into the hot oil. Fry for about 2 minutes, or until golden brown.

4 Remove the mushrooms from the pan with a slotted spoon and drain on kitchen paper (paper towels) while you are cooking the remainder in the same way.

5 Serve hot, sprinkled with coarse salt and garnished with lemon wedges and coriander (cilantro) sprigs.

COOK'S TIP

Gram flour, also known as besan flour, is a pale yellow flour made from chickpeas. It is now readily available from larger supermarkets, as well as Indian food shops and some ethnic delicatessens. Gram flour is also used to make onion bhajis.

Onions à la Grecque

This is a well-known method of cooking vegetables and is perfect with shallots or onions, served with a crisp salad.

NUTRITIONAL INFORMATION	
Calories 200	Sugars 26g
Protein 2g	Fat 9g
Carbohydrate ...28g	Saturates 1g

10 MINS 15 MINS

SERVES 4

INGREDIENTS

- 450 g/1 lb shallots
- 3 tbsp olive oil
- 3 tbsp clear honey
- 2 tbsp garlic wine vinegar
- 3 tbsp dry white wine
- 1 tbsp tomato purée (paste)
- 2 celery stalks, sliced
- 2 tomatoes, seeded and chopped
- salt and pepper
- chopped celery leaves, to garnish

1 Peel the shallots. Heat the oil in a large saucepan, add the shallots and cook, stirring, for 3–5 minutes, or until they begin to brown.

2 Add the honey and cook over a high heat for a further 30 seconds, then add the garlic wine vinegar and dry white wine, stirring well.

3 Stir in the tomato purée (paste), celery and tomatoes and bring the mixture to the boil. Cook over a high heat for 5–6 minutes. Season to taste and leave to cool slightly.

4 Garnish with chopped celery leaves and serve warm. Alternatively chill in the refrigerator before serving.

1

2

3

Cheese, Garlic & Herb Pâté

This wonderful soft cheese pâté is fragrant with the aroma of fresh herbs and garlic. Serve with triangles of Melba toast for a perfect starter.

NUTRITIONAL INFORMATION

Calories	392	Sugars	1g
Protein	17g	Fat	28g
Carbohydrate	18g	Saturates	18g

20 MINS

10 MINS

SERVES 4

INGREDIENTS

- 15 g/½ oz/1 tbsp butter
- 1 garlic clove, crushed
- 3 spring onions (scallions), finely chopped
- 125 g/4½ oz/½ cup full-fat soft cheese
- 2 tbsp chopped mixed herbs, such as parsley, chives, marjoram, oregano and basil
- 175 g/6 oz/1½ cups finely grated mature (sharp) Cheddar cheese
- pepper
- 4–6 slices of white bread from a medium-cut sliced loaf
- mixed salad leaves (greens) and cherry tomatoes, to serve

TO GARNISH

- ground paprika
- herb sprigs

1 Melt the butter in a small frying pan (skillet) and gently fry the garlic and spring onions (scallions) together for 3–4 minutes, until softened. Allow to cool.

2 Beat the soft cheese in a large mixing bowl until smooth, then add the garlic and spring onions (scallions). Stir in the herbs, mixing well.

3 Add the Cheddar and work the mixture together to form a stiff paste. Cover and chill until ready to serve.

4 To make the Melba toast, toast the slices of bread on both sides, and then cut off the crusts. Using a sharp bread knife, cut through the slices horizontally to make very thin slices. Cut into triangles and then lightly grill (broil) the untoasted sides until golden.

5 Arrange the mixed salad leaves (greens) on 4 serving plates with the cherry tomatoes. Pile the cheese pâté on top and sprinkle with a little paprika. Garnish with sprigs of fresh herbs and serve with the Melba toast.

2

3

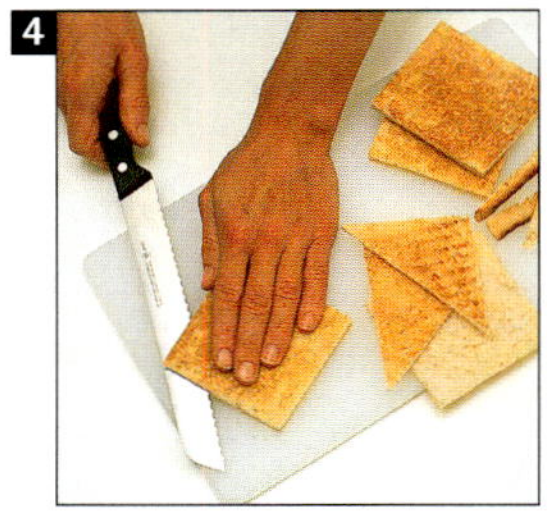
4

Feta Cheese Tartlets

These crisp-baked bread cases, filled with sliced tomatoes, feta cheese, black olives and quail's eggs, are quick to make and taste delicious.

NUTRITIONAL INFORMATION

Calories	570	Sugars	3g
Protein	14g	Fat	42g
Carbohydrate	36g	Saturates	23g

30 MINS 10 MINS

SERVES 4

INGREDIENTS

- 8 slices bread from a medium-cut large loaf
- 125 g/4½ oz/½ cup butter, melted
- 125 g/4½ oz feta cheese, cut into small cubes
- 4 cherry tomatoes, cut into wedges
- 8 pitted black or green olives, halved
- 8 quail's eggs, hard-boiled (hard-cooked)
- 2 tbsp olive oil
- 1 tbsp wine vinegar
- 1 tsp wholegrain mustard
- pinch of caster (superfine) sugar
- salt and pepper
- parsley sprigs, to garnish

1 Remove the crusts from the bread. Trim the bread into squares and flatten each piece with a rolling pin.

2 Brush the bread with melted butter, and then arrange it in bun or muffin tins (pans). Press a piece of crumpled foil into each bread case to secure in place. Bake in a preheated oven, 190°C/375°F/Gas Mark 5, for about 10 minutes, or until crisp and browned.

3 Meanwhile, mix together the feta cheese, tomatoes and olives. Shell the eggs and quarter them. Mix together the olive oil, vinegar, mustard and sugar. Season to taste with salt and pepper.

4 Remove the bread cases from the oven and discard the foil. Leave to cool.

5 Just before serving, f ll the bread cases with the cheese and tomato mixture. Arrange the eggs on top and spoon over the dressing. Garnish with parsley sprigs.

1
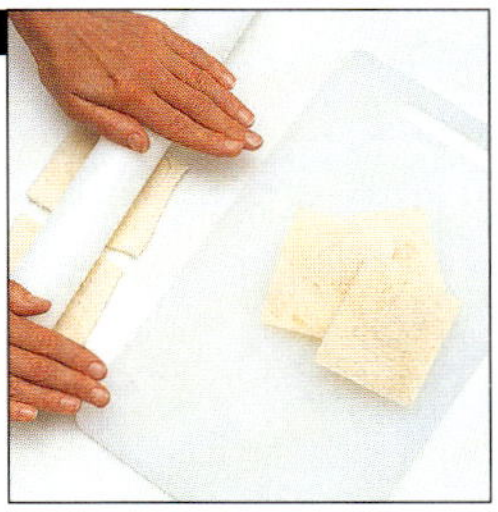

2

5

Mixed Bean Pâté

This is a really quick starter to prepare if canned beans are used. Choose a wide variety of beans for colour and flavour.

NUTRITIONAL INFORMATION	
Calories 126	Sugars 3g
Protein 5g	Fat 6g
Carbohydrate ...13g	Saturates 1g

45 MINS · 0 MINS

SERVES 4

INGREDIENTS

- 400 g/14 oz can mixed beans, drained
- 2 tbsp olive oil
- juice of 1 lemon
- 2 garlic cloves, crushed
- 1 tbsp chopped coriander (cilantro)
- 2 spring onions (scallions), chopped
- salt and pepper
- shredded spring onions (scallions), to garnish

1 Rinse the beans thoroughly under cold running water and drain well.

2 Transfer the beans to a food processor or blender and process until smooth. Alternatively, place the beans in a bowl and mash thoroughly with a fork or potato masher.

3 Add the olive oil, lemon juice, garlic, coriander (cilantro) and spring onions (scallions) and blend until fairly smooth. Season with salt and pepper to taste.

4 Transfer the pâté to a serving bowl and chill in the refrigerator for at least 30 minutes.

5 Garnish with shredded spring onions (scallions) and serve.

2

3

3

Mixed Bhajis

These small bhajis are often served as accompaniments to a main meal, but they are delicious as a starter with a small salad and yogurt sauce.

NUTRITIONAL INFORMATION	
Calories 414	Sugars 7g
Protein 9g	Fat 26g
Carbohydrate ...38g	Saturates 3g

25 MINS   30 MINS

SERVES 4

INGREDIENTS

BHAJIS

- 175 g/6 oz/1¼ cups gram flour
- 1 tsp bicarbonate of soda (baking soda)
- 2 tsp ground coriander
- 1 tsp garam masala
- 1½ tsp turmeric
- 1½ tsp chilli powder
- 2 tbsp chopped coriander (cilantro)
- 1 small onion, halved and sliced
- 1 small leek, sliced
- 100 g/3½ oz cooked cauliflower
- 9-12 tbsp cold water
- salt and pepper
- vegetable oil, for deep-frying

SAUCE

- 150 ml/¼ pint/⅔ cup natural (unsweetened) yogurt
- 2 tbsp chopped mint
- ½ tsp turmeric
- 1 garlic clove, crushed
- mint sprigs, to garnish

1 Sift the flour, bicarbonate of soda (baking soda) and salt to taste into a mixing bowl and add the spices and fresh coriander (cilantro). Mix thoroughly.

1

2

3

2 Divide the mixture into 3 and place in separate bowls. Stir the onion into one bowl, the leek into another and the cauliflower into the third bowl. Add 3–4 tbsp of water to each bowl and mix each to form a smooth paste.

3 Heat the oil for deep-frying in a deep fryer to 180°C/350°F or until a cube of bread browns in 30 seconds. Using 2 dessert spoons, form the mixture into rounds and cook each in the oil for 3–4 minutes, until browned. Remove with a slotted spoon and drain well on absorbent kitchen paper (paper towels). Keep the bhajis warm in the oven while cooking the remainder.

4 Mix all of the sauce ingredients together and pour into a small serving bowl. Garnish with mint sprigs and serve with the warm bhajis.

Garlic Mushrooms on Toast

This is so simple to prepare and looks great if you use a variety of mushrooms for shape and texture.

NUTRITIONAL INFORMATION

Calories	366	Sugars	2g
Protein	9g	Fat	18g
Carbohydrate	45g	Saturates	4g

10 MINS — 10 MINS

SERVES 4

INGREDIENTS

- 75 g/2¾ oz/6 tbsp margarine
- 2 garlic cloves, crushed
- 350 g/12 oz/4 cups mixed mushrooms, such as open-cap, button, oyster and shiitake, sliced
- 8 slices French bread
- 1 tbsp chopped parsley
- salt and pepper

1 Melt the margarine in a frying pan (skillet). Add the crushed garlic and cook, stirring constantly, for 30 seconds.

2 Add the mushrooms and cook, turning occasionally, for 5 minutes.

3 Toast the French bread slices under a preheated medium grill (broiler) for 2–3 minutes, turning once. Transfer the toasts to a serving plate.

2

3

4

4 Toss the parsley into the mushrooms, mixing well, and season well with salt and pepper to taste.

5 Spoon the mushroom mixture over the bread and serve immediately.

COOK'S TIP

Always store mushrooms for a maximum of 24–36 hours in the refrigerator, in paper bags, as they sweat in plastic. Wild mushrooms should be washed but other varieties can simply be wiped with kitchen paper (paper towels).

Corn & Potato Fritters

An ideal supper dish for two, or for one if you halve the quantities. You can use the remaining corn in another recipe.

NUTRITIONAL INFORMATION

Calories	639	Sugars	17g
Protein	28g	Fat	31g
Carbohydrate	65g	Saturates	9g

20 MINS   20 MINS

SERVES 2

INGREDIENTS

- 2 tbsp oil
- 1 small onion, thinly sliced
- 1 garlic clove, crushed
- 350 g/12 oz potatoes
- 200 g/7 oz can of sweetcorn (corn), drained
- ½ tsp dried oregano
- 1 egg, beaten
- 60 g/2 oz/½ cup grated Edam or Gouda cheese
- salt and pepper
- 2–4 eggs
- 2–4 tomatoes, sliced
- parsley sprigs, to garnish

1 Heat 1 tablespoon of the oil in a non-stick frying pan (skillet). Add the onion and garlic and fry very gently, stirring frequently, until soft, but only lightly coloured. Remove from the heat.

2 Grate the potatoes coarsely into a bowl and mix in the sweetcorn (corn), oregano, beaten egg and salt and pepper to taste. Add the fried onion.

3 Heat the remaining oil in the frying pan (skillet). Divide the potato mixture in half and add to the pan (skillet) to make 2 oval-shaped cakes, levelling and shaping the cakes with a palette knife (spatula).

4 Cook the fritters over a low heat for about 10 minutes, until golden brown underneath and almost cooked through, keeping them tidily in shape with the palette knife (spatula) and loosening so they don't stick.

5 Sprinkle each potato fritter with the grated cheese and place under a preheated moderately hot grill (broiler) until golden brown.

6 Meanwhile, poach 1 or 2 eggs for each person until just cooked. Transfer the fritters to warmed plates and top with the eggs and sliced tomatoes. Garnish with parsley and serve at once.

2

4

5

Mixed Bean Pan-Fry

Fresh green beans have a wonderful flavour that is hard to beat. If you cannot find fresh beans, use thawed, frozen beans instead.

1

3

4

NUTRITIONAL INFORMATION

Calories	179	Sugars	4g
Protein	10g	Fat	11g
Carbohydrate	10g	Saturates	1g

10 MINS 15 MINS

SERVES 4

INGREDIENTS

350 g/12 oz/4 cups mixed green beans, such as French (green) and broad (fava) beans, podded
2 tbsp vegetable oil
2 garlic cloves, crushed
1 red onion, halved and sliced
225 g/8 oz firm marinated tofu (bean curd), diced
1 tbsp lemon juice
½ tsp turmeric
1 tsp ground mixed spice
150 ml/¼ pint/⅔ cup vegetable stock
2 tsp sesame seeds

1 Trim and chop the French (green) beans and set aside until required.

2 Heat the oil in a medium frying pan (skillet). Add the garlic and onion and sauté, stirring frequently, over a low heat for 2 minutes.

3 Add the tofu (bean curd) and cook for 2–3 minutes, until just beginning to turn golden brown.

4 Add the French (green) beans and broad (fava) beans. Stir in the lemon juice, turmeric, ground mixed spice and vegetable stock and bring to the boil over a medium heat.

5 Reduce the heat and simmer for 5–7 minutes, or until the beans are tender. Sprinkle with sesame seeds and serve immediately.

VARIATION

Use smoked tofu (bean curd) instead of marinated tofu (bean curd) for an alternative and quite distinctive flavour.

Scrambled Tofu (Bean Curd)

This is a delicious dish which would serve equally well as a light lunch or supper and makes an excellent after-school snack.

NUTRITIONAL INFORMATION

Calories	392	Sugars	6g
Protein	16g	Fat	22g
Carbohydrate	35g	Saturates	4g

5-10 MINS 5 MINS

SERVES 4

INGREDIENTS

- 75 g/2¾ oz/6 tbsp margarine
- 450 g/1 lb marinated, firm tofu (bean curd)
- 1 red onion, chopped
- 1 red (bell) pepper, seeded and chopped
- 4 ciabatta rolls
- 2 tbsp chopped mixed herbs
- salt and pepper
- fresh herbs, to garnish

1 Melt the margarine in a frying pan (skillet) and crumble the tofu (bean curd) into it.

2 Add the onion and (bell) pepper and cook, stirring occasionally, for 3–4 minutes.

1

2

5

3 Meanwhile, slice the ciabatta rolls in half and toast them under a hot grill (broiler) for about 2–3 minutes, turning once.

4 Remove the toasts and transfer to a serving plate.

5 Add the mixed herbs to the tofu (bean curd) mixture, combine and season to taste with salt and pepper.

6 Spoon the tofu (bean curd) mixture on to the toast and garnish with fresh herbs. Serve at once.

COOK'S TIP

Marinated tofu (bean curd) adds extra flavour to this dish. Smoked tofu (bean curd) could be used instead. Rub the cut surface of a garlic clove over the toasted ciabatta rolls for extra flavour.

Refried Beans with Tortillas

Refried beans are a classic Mexican dish and are usually served as an accompaniment. They are, however, delicious served with warm tortillas.

NUTRITIONAL INFORMATION

Calories	519	Sugars	14g
Protein	25g	Fat	28g
Carbohydrate	44g	Saturates	9g

15 MINS 15 MINS

SERVES 4

INGREDIENTS

BEANS

- 2 tbsp olive oil
- 1 onion, finely chopped
- 3 garlic cloves, crushed
- 1 green chilli, chopped
- 400 g/14 oz can red kidney beans, drained
- 400 g/14 oz can pinto beans, drained
- 2 tbsp chopped coriander (cilantro)
- 150 ml/¼ pint/⅔ cup vegetable stock
- 8 wheat tortillas
- 25 g/1 oz/¼ cup grated Cheddar cheese
- salt and pepper

RELISH

- 4 spring onions (scallions), chopped
- 1 red onion, chopped
- 1 green chilli, chopped
- 1 tbsp garlic wine vinegar
- 1 tsp caster (superfine) sugar
- 1 tomato, chopped

2

3

5

1 Heat the oil for the beans in a large frying pan (skillet) over a medium heat. Add the onion and sauté, stirring frequently, for 3–5 minutes. Add the garlic and chilli and cook for 1 minute.

2 Mash the beans with a potato masher and stir into the pan, together with the coriander (cilantro).

3 Stir in the vegetable stock and cook the beans, stirring constantly, for 5 minutes until soft and pulpy.

4 Meanwhile, place the tortillas on a baking tray (cookie sheet) and heat through in a preheated oven, 180°C/350°F/Gas Mark 4, oven for about 1–2 minutes.

5 Mix the relish ingredients together. Spoon the beans into a serving dish and top with the cheese. Season to taste with salt and pepper. Roll the warm tortillas and serve with the onion relish and refried beans.

Buck Rarebit

This substantial version of cheese on toast – a creamy cheese sauce topped with a poached egg – makes a tasty, filling snack.

NUTRITIONAL INFORMATION

Calories	478	Sugars	2g
Protein	29g	Fat	34g
Carbohydrate	14g	Saturates	20g

10 MINS 15–20 MINS

SERVES 4

INGREDIENTS

- 350 g/12 oz mature (sharp) Cheddar
- 125 g/4½ oz Gouda (Dutch), Gruyère or Emmental (Swiss) cheese
- 1 tsp mustard powder
- 1 tsp wholegrain mustard
- 2-4 tbsp brown ale, cider or milk
- ½ tsp vegetarian Worcestershire sauce
- 4 thick slices white or brown bread
- 4 eggs
- salt and pepper

TO GARNISH

- tomato wedges
- watercress sprigs

1 Grate the cheeses and place in a non-stick saucepan.

2 Add the mustards, seasoning, brown ale, cider or milk and vegetarian Worcestershire sauce and mix well.

3 Heat the cheese mixture gently, stirring until it has melted and is completely thick and creamy. Remove from the heat and leave to cool a little.

4 Toast the slices of bread on each side under a preheated grill (broiler) then spread the rarebit mixture evenly over each piece. Put under a moderate grill (broiler) until golden brown and bubbling.

5 Meanwhile, poach the eggs. If using a poacher, grease the cups, heat the water in the pan and, when just boiling, break the eggs into the cups. Cover and simmer for 4-5 minutes until just set. Alternatively, bring about 4 cm/1½ inches of water to the boil in a frying pan (skillet) or large saucepan and for each egg quickly swirl the water with a knife and drop the egg into the "hole" created. Cook for about 4 minutes until just set.

6 Top the rarebits with a poached egg and serve garnished with tomato wedges and sprigs of watercress.

VARIATION

For a change, you can use part or all Stilton or other blue cheese; the appearance is not so attractive but the flavour is very good.

Stuffed Globe Artichokes

This imaginative and attractive recipe for artichokes stuffed with nuts, tomatoes, olives and mushrooms, has been adapted for the microwave.

NUTRITIONAL INFORMATION			
Calories	248	Sugars	8g
Protein	5g	Fat	19g
Carbohydrate	16g	Saturates	2g

30 MINS

25 MINS

SERVES 4

INGREDIENTS

- 4 globe artichokes
- 8 tbsp water
- 4 tbsp lemon juice
- 1 onion, chopped
- 1 garlic clove, crushed
- 2 tbsp olive oil
- 225 g/8 oz/2 cups button mushrooms, chopped
- 40 g/1½ oz/½ cup pitted black olives, sliced
- 60 g/2 oz/¼ cup sun-dried tomatoes in oil, drained and chopped
- 1 tbsp chopped fresh basil
- 60 g/2 oz/1 cup fresh white breadcrumbs
- 25 g/1 oz/¼ cup pine nuts, toasted
- oil from the jar of sun-dried tomatoes for drizzling
- salt and pepper

1 Cut the stalks and lower leaves off the artichokes. Snip off the leaf tips with scissors. Place 2 artichokes in a large bowl with half the water and half the lemon juice. Cover and cook on HIGH power for 10 minutes, turning the artichokes over halfway through, until a leaf pulls away easily from the base. Leave to stand, covered, for 3 minutes before draining. Turn the artichokes upside down and leave to cool. Repeat to cook the remaining artichokes.

2 Place the onion, garlic and oil in a bowl. Cover and cook on HIGH power for 2 minutes, stirring once. Add the mushrooms, olives and sun-dried tomatoes. Cover and cook on HIGH power for 2 minutes.

3 Stir in the basil, breadcrumbs and pine nuts. Season to taste with salt and pepper.

4 Turn the artichokes the right way up and carefully pull the leaves apart. Remove the purple-tipped central leaves. Using a teaspoon, scrape out the hairy choke and discard.

5 Divide the stuffing into 4 equal portions and spoon into the centre of each artichoke. Push the leaves back around the stuffing.

6 Arrange in a shallow dish and drizzle over a little oil from the jar of sun-dried tomatoes. Cook on HIGH power for 7–8 minutes to reheat, turning the artichokes around halfway through.

1

4

5

Three-Cheese Fondue

A hot cheese dip made from three different cheeses can be prepared easily and with guaranteed success in the microwave oven.

NUTRITIONAL INFORMATION	
Calories 565	Sugars 1g
Protein 29g	Fat 38g
Carbohydrate ...15g	Saturates 24g

15 MINS

10 MINS

SERVES 4

INGREDIENTS

- 1 garlic clove
- 300 ml/½ pint/1¼ cups dry white wine
- 250 g/8 oz/2 cups grated mild Cheddar cheese
- 125 g/4½ oz/1 cup grated Gruyère (Swiss) cheese
- 125 g/4½ oz/1 cup grated mozzarella cheese
- 2 tbsp cornflour (cornstarch)
- pepper

TO SERVE

- French bread
- vegetables, such as courgettes (zucchini), mushrooms, baby corn cobs and cauliflower

1 Bruise the garlic by placing the flat side of a knife on top and pressing down with the heel of your hand.

2 Rub the garlic around the inside of a large bowl. Discard the garlic.

3 Pour the wine into the bowl and heat, uncovered, on HIGH power for 3–4 minutes, until hot but not boiling.

4 Gradually add the Cheddar and Gruyère (Swiss) cheeses, stirring well after each addition, then add the mozzarella. Stir until completely melted.

5 Mix the cornflour (cornstarch) with a little water to a smooth paste and stir into the cheese mixture. Season to taste with pepper.

6 Cover and cook on MEDIUM power for 6 minutes, stirring twice during cooking, until the sauce is smooth.

7 Cut the French bread into cubes and the vegetables into batons, slices or florets. To serve, keep the fondue warm over a spirit lamp or reheat as necessary in the microwave oven. Dip in cubes of French bread and batons, slices or florets of vegetables.

3

4

5

COOK'S TIP

Make sure you add the cheese to the wine gradually, mixing well in between each addition, otherwise the mixture might curdle.

Vegetable Kebabs (Kabobs)

These kebabs (kabobs), made from a spicy vegetable mixture, are delightfully easy to make and taste delicious.

NUTRITIONAL INFORMATION			
Calories	268	Sugars	1g
Protein	2g	Fat	25g
Carbohydrate	9g	Saturates	3g

20 MINS   25-30 MINS

MAKES 12

INGREDIENTS

- 2 large potatoes, sliced
- 1 medium onion, sliced
- ½ medium cauliflower, cut into small florets
- 50 g/1¾ oz/ scant ½ cup peas
- 1 tbsp spinach purée (paste)
- 2-3 green chillies
- fresh coriander (cilantro) leaves
- 1 tsp finely chopped root ginger
- 1 tsp crushed garlic
- 1 tsp ground coriander
- 1 pinch turmeric
- 1 tsp salt
- 60 g/1¾ oz/1 cup breadcrumbs
- 300 ml/½ pint/1¼ cups vegetable oil
- fresh chilli strips, to garnish

1 Place the potatoes, onion and cauliflower florets in a pan of water and bring to the boil. Reduce the heat and simmer until the potatoes are cooked through. Remove the vegetables from the pan with a slotted spoon and drain thoroughly. Set aside.

2 Add the peas and spinach to the vegetables and mix, mashing down thoroughly with a fork.

3 Using a sharp knife, finely chop the green chillies and fresh coriander (cilantro) leaves.

4 Mix the chillies and coriander (cilantro) with the ginger, garlic, ground coriander, turmeric and salt.

5 Blend the spice mixture into the vegetables, mixing with a fork to make a paste.

6 Scatter the breadcrumbs on to a large plate.

7 Break off 10-12 small balls from the spice paste. Flatten them with the palm of your hand to make flat, round shapes.

8 Dip each kebab (kabob) in the breadcrumbs, coating well.

9 Heat the oil in a heavy-based frying-pan (skillet) and shallow-fry the kabobs (kabobs), in batches, until golden brown, turning occasionally. Transfer to serving plates and garnish with fresh chilli strips. Serve hot.

1

2

3

Vegetable Hash

This is a quick one-pan dish which is ideal for a snack. Packed with colour and flavour it is very versatile, as you can add other vegetables.

NUTRITIONAL INFORMATION

Calories	182	Sugars	6g
Protein	5g	Fat	4g
Carbohydrate	34g	Saturates	0.5g

15 MINS — 30 MINS

SERVES 4

INGREDIENTS

- 675 g/1½ lb potatoes, cubed
- 1 tbsp olive oil
- 2 garlic cloves, crushed
- 1 green (bell) pepper, seeded and cubed
- 1 yellow (bell) pepper, seeded and cubed
- 3 tomatoes, diced
- 75 g/2¾ oz/1 cup button mushrooms, halved
- 1 tbsp vegetarian Worcestershire sauce
- 2 tbsp chopped basil
- salt and pepper
- basil sprigs, to garnish
- warm, crusty bread, to serve

1 Cook the potatoes in a saucepan of boiling salted water for 7–8 minutes. Drain well and reserve.

2 Heat the olive oil in a large, heavy-based frying pan (skillet). Add the potatoes and cook, stirring constantly, for 8–10 minutes, until browned.

3 Add the garlic and (bell) peppers and cook, stirring frequently, for 2–3 minutes.

4 Stir in the tomatoes and mushrooms and cook, stirring frequently, for 5–6 minutes.

5 Stir in the vegetarian Worcestershire sauce and basil and season to taste with salt and pepper. Transfer to a warm serving dish, garnish with basil sprigs and serve with warm crusty bread.

COOK'S TIP

Most brands of Worcestershire sauce contain anchovies, so check the label to make sure you choose a vegetarian variety.

Falafel

These are a very tasty, well-known Middle Eastern dish of small chickpea (garbanzo bean) based balls, spiced and deep-fried.

NUTRITIONAL INFORMATION

Calories	491	Sugars	3g
Protein	15g	Fat	30g
Carbohydrate	43g	Saturates	3g

25 MINS 10–15 MINS

SERVES 4

INGREDIENTS

675 g/1½ lb/6 cups canned chickpeas (garbanzo beans), drained

1 red onion, chopped

3 garlic cloves, crushed

100 g/3½ oz wholemeal (whole wheat) bread

2 small fresh red chillies

1 tsp ground cumin

1 tsp ground coriander

½ tsp turmeric

1 tbsp chopped coriander (cilantro), plus extra to garnish

1 egg, beaten

100 g/3½ oz/1 cup wholemeal (whole wheat) breadcrumbs

vegetable oil, for deep-frying

salt and pepper

tomato and cucumber salad and lemon wedges, to serve

1 Put the chickpeas (garbanzo beans), onion, garlic, bread, chillies, spices and coriander (cilantro) in a food processor and process for 30 seconds. Stir and season to taste with salt and pepper.

2

3

4

2 Remove the mixture from the food processor and shape into walnut-sized balls.

3 Place the beaten egg in a shallow bowl and place the wholemeal (whole wheat) breadcrumbs on a plate. Dip the balls first into the egg to coat and then roll them in the breadcrumbs, shaking off any excess.

4 Heat the oil for deep-frying to 180°C/350°F or until a cube of bread browns in 30 seconds. Fry the falafel, in batches if necessary, for 2–3 minutes, until crisp and browned. Remove from the oil with a slotted spoon and dry on absorbent kitchen paper (paper towels). Garnish with coriander (cilantro) and serve with a tomato and cucumber salad and lemon wedges.

Chow Mein

Egg noodles are cooked and then fried with a colourful variety of vegetables to make this well-known and ever-popular dish.

NUTRITIONAL INFORMATION	
Calories 669	Sugars 9g
Protein 19g	Fat 23g
Carbohydrate ..100g	Saturates 4g

15 MINS — 10 MINS

SERVES 4

INGREDIENTS

- 500 g/1 lb 2 oz egg noodles
- 4 tbsp vegetable oil
- 1 onion, thinly sliced
- 2 carrots, cut into thin sticks
- 125 g/4½ oz/1⅓ cups button mushrooms, quartered
- 125 g/4½ oz mangetout (snow peas)
- ½ cucumber, cut into sticks
- 125 g/4½ oz/2 cups spinach, shredded
- 125 g/4½ oz/2 cups beansprouts
- 2 tbsp dark soy sauce
- 1 tbsp sherry
- 1 tsp salt
- 1 tsp sugar
- 1 tsp cornflour (cornstarch)
- 1 tsp sesame oil

2

4

5

1 Cook the noodles according to the instructions on the packet. Drain and rinse under cold running water until cool. Set aside.

2 Heat 3 tablespoons of the vegetable oil in a preheated wok or frying pan (skillet). Add the onion and carrots, and stir-fry for 1 minute. Add the mushrooms, mangetout (snow peas) and cucumber and stir-fry for 1 minute.

3 Stir in the remaining vegetable oil and add the drained noodles, together with the spinach and beansprouts.

4 Blend together all the remaining ingredients and pour over the noodles and vegetables.

5 Stir-fry until the noodle mixture is thoroughly heated through, transfer to a warm serving dish and serve.

COOK'S TIP

For a spicy hot chow mein, add 1 tablespoon chilli sauce or substitute chilli oil for the sesame oil.

Spicy Japanese Noodles

These noodles are highly spiced with chilli and flavoured with sesame seeds for a nutty taste that is a true delight.

2

4

5

NUTRITIONAL INFORMATION			
Calories	381	Sugars	12g
Protein	11g	Fat	13g
Carbohydrate	59g	Saturates	2g

5 MINS   15 MINS

SERVES 4

INGREDIENTS

500 g/1 lb 2 oz fresh Japanese noodles

1 tbsp sesame oil

1 tbsp sesame seeds

1 tbsp sunflower oil

1 red onion, sliced

100 g/3½ oz mangetout, (snow peas)

175 g/6 oz carrots, thinly sliced

350 g/12 oz white cabbage, shredded

3 tbsp sweet chilli sauce

2 spring onions (scallions), sliced, to garnish

1 Bring a large saucepan of water to the boil. Add the Japanese noodles to the pan and cook for 2–3 minutes. Drain the noodles thoroughly.

2 Toss the noodles with the sesame oil and sesame seeds.

3 Heat the sunflower oil in a large preheated wok.

4 Add the onion slices, mangetout (snow peas), carrot slices and shredded cabbage to the wok and stir-fry for about 5 minutes.

5 Add the sweet chilli sauce to the wok and cook, stirring occasionally, for a further 2 minutes.

6 Add the sesame noodles to the wok, toss thoroughly to combine and heat through for a further 2–3 minutes. (You may wish to serve the noodles separately, so transfer them to the serving bowls.)

7 Transfer the Japanese noodles and spicy vegetables to warm individual serving bowls, scatter over the sliced spring onions (scallions) to garnish and serve immediately.

COOK'S TIP

If fresh Japanese noodles are difficult to get hold of, use dried rice noodles or thin egg noodles instead.

Risotto Verde

Risotto is an Italian dish which is easy to make and uses arborio rice, onion and garlic as a base for a range of savoury recipes.

NUTRITIONAL INFORMATION

Calories	374	Sugars	5g
Protein	10g	Fat	9g
Carbohydrate	55g	Saturates	2g

5 MINS — 35 MINS

SERVES 4

INGREDIENTS

- 1.75 litres/3 pints/7½ cups vegetable stock
- 2 tbsp olive oil
- 2 garlic cloves, crushed
- 2 leeks, shredded
- 225 g/8 oz/1¼ cups arborio rice
- 300 ml/½ pint/1¼ cups dry white wine
- 4 tbsp chopped mixed herbs
- 225 g/8 oz baby spinach
- 3 tbsp natural (unsweetened) yogurt
- salt and pepper
- shredded leek, to garnish

1 Pour the stock into a large saucepan and bring to the boil. Reduce the heat to a simmer.

2 Meanwhile, heat the oil in a separate pan. Add the garlic and leeks and sauté over a low heat, stirring occasionally, for 2–3 minutes, until softened.

3 Stir in the rice and cook for 2 minutes, stirring until each grain is coated with oil.

4 Pour in half of the wine and a little of the hot stock. Cook over a low heat until all of the liquid has been absorbed. Add the remaining stock and the wine, a little at a time, and cook over a low heat for 25 minutes, or until the rice is creamy.

5 Stir in the chopped mixed herbs and baby spinach, season to taste with salt and pepper and cook for 2 minutes.

6 Stir in the natural (unsweetened) yogurt. Transfer to a warm serving dish, garnish with the shredded leek and serve immediately.

2

4

5

COOK'S TIP

Do not try to hurry the process of cooking the risotto as the rice must absorb the liquid slowly in order for it to reach the correct consistency.

Special Fried Rice

In this simple recipe, cooked rice is fried with vegetables and cashew nuts. It can either be eaten on its own or served as an accompaniment.

NUTRITIONAL INFORMATION

Calories	355	Sugars	6g
Protein	9g	Fat	15g
Carbohydrate	48g	Saturates	3g

10 MINS

30 MINS

SERVES 4

INGREDIENTS

175 g/6 oz/generous ¾ cup long grain rice

60 g/2 oz/½ cup cashew nuts

1 carrot

½ cucumber

1 yellow (bell) pepper

2 spring onions (scallions)

2 tbsp vegetable oil

1 garlic clove, crushed

125 g/4½ oz/¾ cup frozen peas, thawed

1 tbsp soy sauce

1 tsp salt

coriander (cilantro) leaves, to garnish

1 Bring a large pan of water to the boil. Add the rice and simmer for 15 minutes. Tip the rice into a strainer and rinse; drain thoroughly.

2 Heat a wok or large, heavy-based frying pan (skillet), add the cashew nuts and dry-fry until lightly browned. Remove and set aside.

3 Cut the carrot in half along the length, then slice thinly into semi-circles. Halve the cucumber and remove the seeds, using a teaspoon, then dice the flesh. Seed and slice the (bell) pepper and chop the spring onions (scallions).

4 Heat the oil in a wok or large frying pan (skillet). Add the prepared vegetables and the garlic. Stir-fry for 3 minutes. Add the rice, peas, soy sauce and salt. Continue to stir-fry until well mixed and thoroughly heated.

5 Stir in the reserved cashew nuts. Transfer to a warmed serving dish, garnish with coriander (cilantro) leaves and serve immediately.

COOK'S TIP

You can replace any of the vegetables in this recipe with others suitable for a stir-fry, and using leftover rice makes this a perfect last-minute dish.

Kitchouri

The traditional breakfast plate of kedgeree reputedly has its roots in this Indian flavoured rice dish, which English colonists adopted.

NUTRITIONAL INFORMATION	
Calories 318	Sugars 5g
Protein 12g	Fat 10g
Carbohydrate . . .48g	Saturates 6g

10 MINS | 30 MINS

SERVES 4

INGREDIENTS

- 2 tbsp vegetable ghee or butter
- 1 red onion, finely chopped
- 1 garlic clove, crushed
- ½ celery stick, finely chopped
- 1 tsp turmeric
- ½ tsp garam masala
- 1 green chilli, seeded and finely chopped
- ½ tsp cumin seeds
- 1 tbsp chopped coriander (cilantro)
- 125 g/4½ oz/generous ½ cup basmati rice, rinsed under cold water
- 125 g/4½ oz/½ cup green lentils
- 300 ml/½ pint/1¼ cups vegetable juice
- 600 ml/1 pint/2½ cups vegetable stock

1 Heat the ghee or butter in a large heavy-based saucepan. Add the onion, garlic and celery and cook for about 5 minutes, until soft.

2 Add the turmeric, garam masala, green chilli, cumin seeds and coriander (cilantro). Cook over a moderate heat, stirring constantly, for about 1 minute, until fragrant.

3 Add the rice and lentils and cook for 1 minute, until the rice is translucent.

4 Pour the vegetable juice and stock into the saucepan and bring to the boil over a medium heat. Cover and simmer over a low heat, stirring occasionally, for about 20 minutes, or until the lentils are cooked. (They should be tender when pressed between two fingers.)

5 Transfer the kitchouri to a warmed serving dish and serve piping hot.

COOK'S TIP

This is a versatile dish, and can be served as a great-tasting and satisfying one-pot meal. It can also be served as a winter lunch dish with tomatoes and yogurt.

Midweek Medley

Canned chickpeas (garbanzo beans) are used in this dish, but you could use black-eye beans (peas) or red kidney beans, if preferred.

NUTRITIONAL INFORMATION			
Calories	480	Sugars	8g
Protein	11g	Fat	38g
Carbohydrate	25g	Saturates	13g

15 MINS — 20-25 MINS

SERVES 4

INGREDIENTS

- 1 large aubergine (eggplant)
- 2 courgettes (zucchini)
- 6 tbsp vegetable ghee or oil
- 1 large onion, quartered and sliced
- 2 garlic cloves, crushed
- 1-2 fresh green chillies, seeded and chopped, or 1-2 tsp minced chilli
- 2 tsp ground coriander
- 2 tsp cumin seeds
- 1 tsp ground turmeric
- 1 tsp garam masala
- 400 g/14 oz can chopped tomatoes
- 300 ml/½pint/1¼ cups vegetable stock or water
- salt and pepper
- 400 g/14 oz can chickpeas (garbanzo beans), drained and rinsed
- 2 tbsp chopped mint
- 150 ml/¼ pint/⅔ cup double (heavy) cream

1 Trim the leaf end off the aubergine (eggplant) and cut into cubes. Trim and slice the courgettes (zucchini).

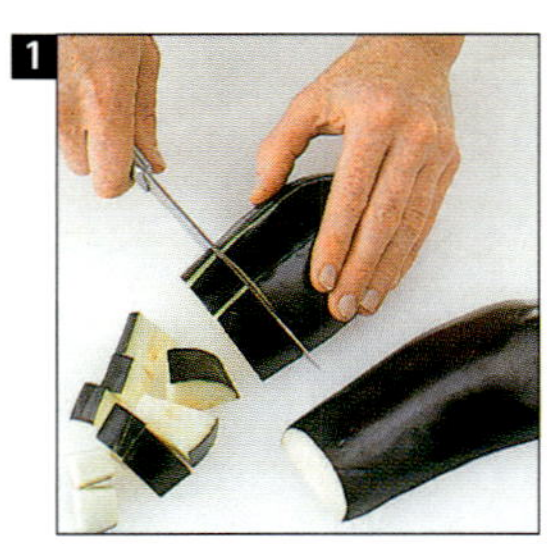

2 Heat the ghee or oil in a saucepan and fry the aubergine (eggplant), courgettes (zucchini), onion, garlic and chillies over a low heat, stirring frequently, for about 5 minutes, adding a little more oil to the pan, if necessary.

3 Stir in the spices and cook for 30 seconds. Add the tomatoes and stock and season with salt and pepper to taste. Cook for 10 minutes.

4 Add the chickpeas (garbanzo beans) to the pan and cook for a further 5 minutes.

5 Stir in the mint and cream and reheat gently. Taste and adjust the seasoning, if necessary. Transfer to a warm serving dish and serve hot with plain or pilau rice, or with parathas, if preferred.

Spiced Rice & Lentils

This is a lovely combination of rice and masoor dhal and is simple to cook. You can add a knob of unsalted butter before serving, if liked.

NUTRITIONAL INFORMATION

Calories	394	Sugars	3g
Protein	14g	Fat	8g
Carbohydrate	70g	Saturates	1g

5 MINS   30 MINS

SERVES 4

INGREDIENTS

- 200 g/7 oz/1 cup basmati rice
- 175 g/6 oz/¾ cup masoor dhal
- 2 tbsp vegetable ghee
- 1 small onion, sliced
- 1 tsp finely chopped root ginger
- 1 tsp crushed garlic
- ½ tsp turmeric
- 600 ml/1 pint/2½ cups water
- 1 tsp salt

1 Combine the rice and dhal and rinse thoroughly in cold running water. Set aside until required.

2 Heat the ghee in a large saucepan. Add the onion and fry, stirring occasionally, for about 2 minutes.

3 Reduce the heat, add the ginger, garlic, and turmeric and stir-fry for 1 minute.

4 Add the rice and dhal to the mixture in the pan and blend together, mixing gently, but thoroughly.

5 Add the water to the mixture in the pan and bring to the boil over a medium heat. Reduce the heat, cover and cook for 20–25 minutes, until the rice is tender and the liquid is absorbed.

6 Just before serving, add the salt and mix to combine.

7 Transfer the spiced rice and lentils to a large warmed serving dish and serve immediately.

COOK'S TIP

Many Indian recipes specify using ghee as the cooking fat. This is because it is similar to clarified butter in that it can be heated to a very high temperature without burning. Ghee adds a nutty flavour to dishes and a glossy shine to sauces.

Thai Jasmine Rice

Every Thai meal has as its centrepiece a big bowl of steaming, fluffy Thai jasmine rice, to which salt should not be added.

NUTRITIONAL INFORMATION

Calories	239	Sugars	0g
Protein	5g	Fat	2g
Carbohydrate	54g	Saturates	0.6g

5 MINS

10-15 MINS

SERVES 4

INGREDIENTS

OPEN PAN METHOD

225 g/8 oz/generous 1 cup Thai jasmine rice

1 litre/1¾ pints/4 cups water

ABSORPTION METHOD

225 g/8 oz/generous 1 cup Thai jasmine rice

450 ml/16 fl oz/scant 2 cups water

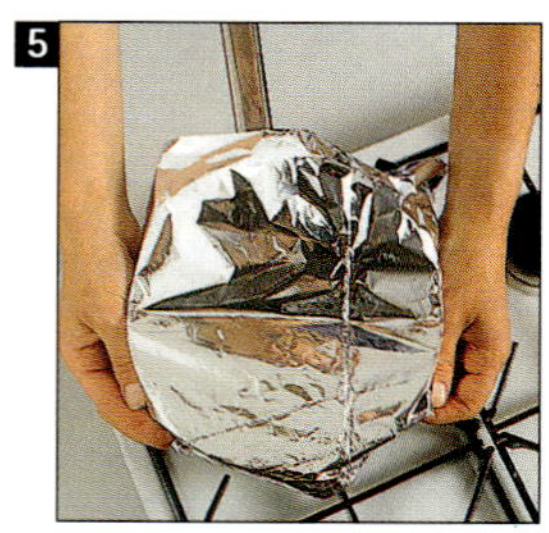

1 For the open pan method, rinse the rice in a strainer under cold running water and leave to drain.

2 Bring the water to the boil. Add the rice, stir once and return to a medium boil. Cook, uncovered, for 8–10 minutes, until tender.

3 Drain thoroughly and fork through lightly before serving.

4 For the absorption method, rinse the rice under cold running water.

5 Put the rice and water into a saucepan and bring to the boil. Stir once and then cover the pan tightly. Lower the heat as much as possible. Cook for 10 minutes. Leave to rest for 5 minutes.

6 Fork through lightly and serve the rice immediately.

COOK'S TIP

Thai jasmine rice can be frozen. Freeze in a plastic sealed container. Frozen rice is ideal for stir-fry dishes, as the process seems to separate the grains.

White Lentils

This dhal is dry when cooked, so give it a baghaar (seasoned oil) dressing. It makes an excellent accompaniment to any meal of kormas.

NUTRITIONAL INFORMATION

Calories	129	Sugars	1g
Protein	6g	Fat	6g
Carbohydrate	14g	Saturates	1g

5 MINS 45 MINS

SERVES 4

INGREDIENTS

- 100 g/3½ oz/½ cup urid dhal
- 1 tsp finely chopped root ginger
- 600 ml/1 pint/2½ cups water
- 1 tsp salt
- 1 tsp pepper
- 2 tbsp vegetable ghee
- 2 garlic cloves
- 2 fresh red chillies, finely chopped
- mint leaves, to garnish
- chapatis, to serve

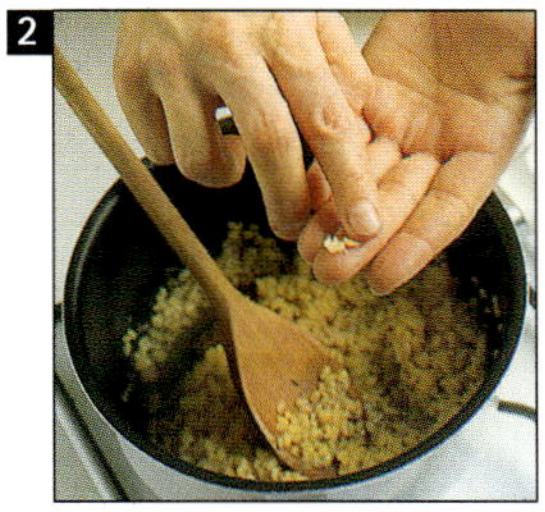

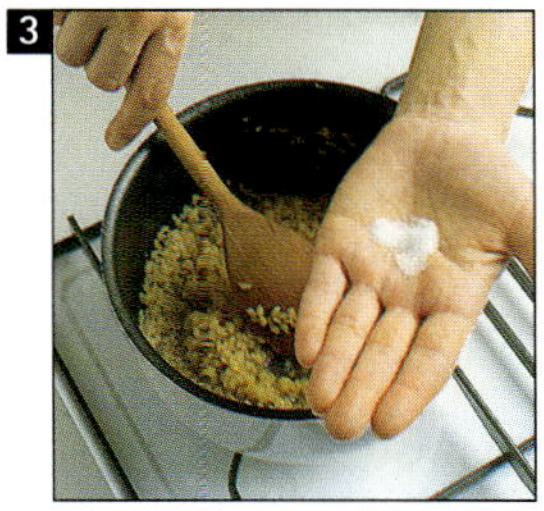

1 Rinse the lentils thoroughly and put them in a large saucepan, together with the ginger.

2 Add the water and bring to a boil. Cover and simmer over a medium heat for about 30 minutes. Check to see whether the lentils are cooked by rubbing them between your finger and thumb. If they are still a little hard in the middle, cook for a further 5–7 minutes. If necessary, remove the lid and cook until any remaining water has evaporated.

3 Add the salt and pepper to the lentils, mix well and set aside.

4 To make the baghaar, heat the ghee in a separate saucepan. Add the cloves of garlic and chopped red chillies and stir well to mix thoroughly.

5 Pour the garlic and chilli mixture over the lentils and then garnish with the fresh mint leaves.

6 Transfer the white lentils to warm individual serving dishes and serve hot with chapatis .

COOK'S TIP

Ghee was traditionally made from clarified butter, which can withstand higher temperatures than ordinary butter. Vegetable ghee has largely replaced it now because it is lower in saturated fats.

Deep South Rice & Beans

Cajun spices add a flavour of the American Deep South to this colourful rice and red kidney bean salad.

NUTRITIONAL INFORMATION			
Calories	336	Sugars	8g
Protein	7g	Fat	13g
Carbohydrate	51g	Saturates	2g

10 MINS 15 MINS

SERVES 4

INGREDIENTS

- 175 g/6 oz/scant 1 cup long grain rice
- 4 tbsp olive oil
- 1 small green (bell) pepper, seeded and chopped
- 1 small red (bell) pepper, seeded and chopped
- 1 onion, finely chopped
- 1 small red or green chilli, seeded and finely chopped
- 2 tomatoes, chopped
- 125 g/4½ oz/½ cup canned red kidney beans, rinsed and drained
- 1 tbsp chopped fresh basil
- 2 tsp chopped fresh thyme
- 1 tsp Cajun spice
- salt and pepper
- fresh basil leaves, to garnish

1 Cook the rice in plenty of boiling, lightly salted water for about 12 minutes, until just tender. Rinse with cold water and drain well.

2 Meanwhile, heat the olive oil in a frying pan (skillet) and fry the green and red (bell) peppers and onion gently for about 5 minutes, until softened.

3 Add the chilli and tomatoes, and cook for a further 2 minutes.

4 Add the vegetable mixture and red kidney beans to the rice. Stir well to combine thoroughly.

5 Stir the chopped herbs and Cajun spice into the rice mixture. Season to taste with salt and pepper, and serve, garnished with basil leaves.

Onion Dhal

This dhal is semi-dry when cooked, so it is best to serve it with a dish which has a sauce. Ordinary onions can be used as a substitute.

NUTRITIONAL INFORMATION

Calories	232	Sugars	1g
Protein	6g	Fat	17g
Carbohydrate	15g	Saturates	2g

5 MINS 30 MINS

SERVES 4

INGREDIENTS

- 100 g/3½ oz/½ cup masoor dhal
- 6 tbsp vegetable oil
- 1 small bunch spring onions (scallions), chopped
- 1 tsp finely chopped root ginger
- 1 tsp crushed garlic
- ½ tsp chilli powder
- ½ tsp turmeric
- 300 ml/½ pint/1¼ cups water
- 1 tsp salt
- 1 fresh green chilli, finely chopped
- fresh coriander (cilantro) leaves

2

3

3

1 Rinse the lentils thoroughly and set aside until required.

2 Heat the oil in a heavy-based saucepan. Add the spring onions (scallions) to the pan and fry over a medium heat, stirring frequently, until lightly browned.

3 Reduce the heat and add the ginger, garlic, chilli powder and turmeric. Briefly stir-fry the spring onions (scallions) with the spices. Add the lentils and mix to blend together.

4 Add the water to the lentil mixture, reduce the heat to low and cook for 20–25 minutes.

5 When the lentils are cooked thoroughly, add the salt and stir gently to mix well.

6 Transfer the onion lentils to a serving dish. Garnish with the chopped green chillies and fresh coriander (cilantro) leaves and serve immediately.

COOK'S TIP

Masoor dhal are small, round, pale orange split lentils. They turn a pale yellow colour when cooked.

Bulgur Pilau

Bulgur wheat is very easy to use and, as well as being full of nutrients, it is a delicious alternative to rice, having a distinctive nutty flavour.

NUTRITIONAL INFORMATION

Calories	637	Sugars	25g
Protein	16g	Fat	26g
Carbohydrate	90g	Saturates	11g

15 MINS — 35–40 MINS

SERVES 4

INGREDIENTS

- 75 g/2¾ oz/6 tbsp butter or margarine
- 1 red onion, halved and sliced
- 2 garlic cloves, crushed
- 350 g/12 oz/2 cups bulgur wheat
- 175 g/6 oz tomatoes, seeded and chopped
- 50 g/1¾ oz baby corn cobs, halved lengthways
- 75 g/2¾ oz small broccoli florets
- 850 ml/1½ pints/3¾ cups vegetable stock
- 2 tbsp clear honey
- 50 g/1¾ oz sultanas (golden raisins)
- 50 g/1¾ oz/½ cup pine nuts
- ½ tsp ground cinnamon
- ½ tsp ground cumin
- salt and pepper
- sliced spring onions (scallions), to garnish

2

3

4

1 Melt the butter or margarine in a large flameproof casserole.

2 Add the onion and garlic and sauté for 2–3 minutes, stirring occasionally.

3 Add the bulgur wheat, tomatoes, corn cobs, broccoli and stock and bring to the boil. Reduce the heat, cover and cook, stirring occasionally, for 15–20 minutes.

4 Stir in the honey, sultanas (golden raisins), pine nuts, ground cinnamon and cumin and season with salt and pepper to taste, mixing well. Remove the casserole from the heat, cover and set aside for 10 minutes.

5 Spoon the bulgur pilau into a warmed serving dish.

6 Garnish the bulgur pilau with thinly sliced spring onions (scallions) and serve immediately.

COOK'S TIP

The dish is left to stand for 10 minutes so that the bulgur can finish cooking and the flavours will mingle.

Vegballs with Chilli Sauce

These tasty, nutty morsels are delicious served with a fiery, tangy sauce that counteracts the richness of the peanuts.

NUTRITIONAL INFORMATION			
Calories	615	Sugars	13g
Protein	23g	Fat	43g
Carbohydrate	37g	Saturates	8g

25 MINS 30 MINS

SERVES 4

INGREDIENTS

- 3 tbsp groundnut oil
- 1 onion, finely chopped
- 1 celery stalk, chopped
- 1 tsp dried mixed herbs
- 225 g/8 oz/2 cups roasted unsalted peanuts, ground
- 175 g/6 oz/1 cup canned chickpeas (garbanzo beans), drained and mashed
- 1 tsp yeast extract
- 60 g/2 oz/1 cup fresh wholemeal (whole wheat) breadcrumbs
- 1 egg yolk
- 25 g/1 oz/¼ cup plain (all-purpose) flour
- strips of fresh red chilli, to garnish

HOT CHILLI SAUCE

- 2 tsp groundnut oil
- 1 large red chilli, seeded and finely chopped
- 2 spring onions (scallions), finely chopped
- 2 tbsp red wine vinegar
- 200 g/7 oz can chopped tomatoes
- 2 tbsp tomato purée (paste)
- 2 tsp caster (superfine) sugar
- salt and pepper
- rice and green salad (salad greens), to serve

1 Heat 1 tablespoon of the oil in a frying pan (skillet) and gently fry the onion and celery for 3–4 minutes, until softened, but not browned.

2 Place all the other ingredients, except the remaining oil and the flour, in a mixing bowl and add the onion and celery. Mix well.

3 Divide the mixture into 12 portions and roll into small balls. Coat all over with the flour.

4 Heat the remaining oil in a frying pan (skillet). Add the chickpea (garbanzo bean) balls and cook over a medium heat, turning frequently, for 15 minutes, until cooked through and golden. Drain on kitchen paper (paper towels).

5 Meanwhile, make the hot chilli sauce. Heat the oil in a small frying pan (skillet) and gently fry the chilli and spring onions (scallions) for 2–3 minutes. Stir in the remaining ingredients and season. Bring to the boil and simmer for 5 minutes.

6 Serve the chickpea (garbanzo bean) and peanut balls with the hot chilli sauce, rice and a salad.

2

3

4

Creamy Vegetable Curry

Vegetables are cooked in a mildly spiced curry sauce with yogurt and fresh coriander (cilantro) stirred in just before serving.

NUTRITIONAL INFORMATION			
Calories	423	Sugars	24g
Protein	16g	Fat	19g
Carbohydrate	50g	Saturates	7g

20 MINS 25 MINS

SERVES 4

INGREDIENTS

- 2 tbsp sunflower oil
- 1 onion, sliced
- 2 tsp cumin seeds
- 2 tbsp ground coriander
- 1 tsp ground turmeric
- 2 tsp ground ginger
- 1 tsp chopped fresh red chilli
- 2 garlic cloves, chopped
- 400 g/14 oz can chopped tomatoes
- 3 tbsp powdered coconut mixed with 300 ml/½ pint/1¼ cups boiling water
- 1 small cauliflower, broken into florets
- 2 courgettes (zucchini), sliced
- 2 carrots, sliced
- 1 potato, diced
- 400 g/14 oz can chickpeas (garbanzo beans), drained and rinsed
- 150 ml/¼ pint/¾ cup thick natural (unsweetened) yogurt
- 2 tbsp mango chutney
- 3 tbsp chopped fresh coriander (cilantro)
- salt and pepper
- fresh herbs, to garnish

1

3

4

1 Heat the oil in a saucepan and fry the onion until softened. Add the cumin, ground coriander, turmeric, ginger, chilli and garlic and fry for 1 minute.

2 Add the tomatoes and coconut mixture and mix well.

3 Add the cauliflower florets, courgettes (zucchini), carrots, diced potato and chickpeas (garbanzo beans) and season to taste with salt and pepper. Cover and simmer for 20 minutes, until the vegetables are tender.

4 Stir in the yogurt, mango chutney and fresh coriander (cilantro) and heat through gently, but do not boil. Transfer to a warm serving dish, garnish with fresh herbs and serve.

Red Curry with Cashews

This is a wonderfully quick dish to prepare. If you don't have time to prepare the curry paste, it can be bought ready-made.

NUTRITIONAL INFORMATION

Calories	274	Sugars	5g
Protein	10g	Fat	10g
Carbohydrate	38g	Saturates	3g

25 MINS 15 MINS

SERVES 4

INGREDIENTS

- 250 ml/9 fl oz/1 cup coconut milk
- 1 kaffir lime leaf
- ¼ tsp light soy sauce
- 60 g/2 oz/4 baby corn cobs, halved lengthways
- 125 g/4½ oz/1¼ cups broccoli florets
- 125 g/4½ oz French (green) beans, cut into 5 cm/2 inch pieces
- 25 g/1 oz/¼ cup cashew nuts
- 15 fresh basil leaves
- 1 tbsp chopped coriander (cilantro)
- 1 tbsp chopped roast peanuts, to garnish

RED CURRY PASTE

- 7 fresh red chillies, halved, seeded and blanched
- 2 tsp cumin seeds
- 2 tsp coriander seeds
- 2.5 cm/1 inch piece galangal, chopped
- ½ stalk lemon grass, chopped
- 1 tsp salt
- grated rind of 1 lime
- 4 garlic cloves, chopped
- 3 shallots, chopped
- 2 kaffir lime leaves, shredded
- 1 tbsp vegetable oil

1 To make the curry paste, grind all the ingredients together in a large mortar with a pestle or a grinder. Alternatively, process briefly in a food processor. The quantity of red curry paste is more than required for this recipe. However, it will keep for up to 3 weeks in a sealed container in the refrigerator.

1

2 Put a wok or large, heavy-based frying pan (skillet) over a high heat, add 3 tablespoons of the red curry paste and stir until it gives off its aroma. Reduce the heat to medium.

3 Add the coconut milk, kaffir lime leaf, light soy sauce, baby corn cobs, broccoli florets, French (green) beans and cashew nuts. Bring to the boil and simmer for about 10 minutes, until the vegetables are cooked, but still firm and crunchy.

3

4 Remove and discard the lime leaf and stir in the basil leaves and coriander (cilantro). Transfer to a warmed serving dish, garnish with peanuts and serve immediately.

4

Sauté of Summer Vegetables

The freshness of lightly cooked summer vegetables is enhanced by the aromatic flavour of a tarragon and white wine dressing.

NUTRITIONAL INFORMATION

Calories	217	Sugars	8g
Protein	2g	Fat	18g
Carbohydrate	9g	Saturates	9g

10 MINS 10–15 MINS

SERVES 4

INGREDIENTS

225 g/8 oz baby carrots, scrubbed
125 g/4½ oz runner (string) beans
2 courgettes (zucchini), trimmed
1 bunch large spring onions (scallions)
1 bunch radishes
60 g/2 oz/½ cup butter
2 tbsp light olive oil
2 tbsp white wine vinegar
4 tbsp dry white wine
1 tsp caster (superfine) sugar
1 tbsp chopped tarragon
salt and pepper
tarragon sprigs, to garnish

1 Cut the carrots in half lengthways, slice the beans and courgettes (zucchini), and halve the spring onions (scallions) and radishes, so that all the vegetables are cut to even-size pieces.

2 Melt the butter in a large, heavy-based frying pan (skillet) or wok. Add all the vegetables and fry them over a medium heat, stirring frequently, until they are tender, but still crisp and firm to the bite.

1

2

4

3 Heat the olive oil, vinegar, white wine and sugar in a small saucepan over a low heat, stirring until the sugar has dissolved. Remove from the heat and add the chopped tarragon.

4 When the vegetables are just cooked, pour over the 'dressing'. Stir through, tossing the vegetables to coat well, and then transfer to a warmed serving dish. Garnish with sprigs of fresh tarragon and serve at once.

Creamy Baked Fennel

Fennel tastes fabulous in this creamy sauce, flavoured with caraway seeds. A crunchy breadcrumb topping gives an interesting texture.

1

2

4

NUTRITIONAL INFORMATION

Calories	292	Sugars	5g
Protein	10g	Fat	23g
Carbohydrate	12g	Saturates	14g

10 MINS 45 MINS

SERVES 4

INGREDIENTS

- 2 tbsp lemon juice
- 2 fennel bulbs, thinly sliced
- 60 g/2 oz/¼ cup butter, plus extra for greasing
- 125 g/4½ oz/¼ cup low-fat soft cheese
- 150 ml/¼ pint/⅔ cup single (light) cream
- 150 ml/¼ pint/⅔ cup milk
- 1 egg, beaten
- 2 tsp caraway seeds
- 60 g/2 oz/1 cup fresh white breadcrumbs
- salt and pepper
- parsley sprigs, to garnish

1 Bring a saucepan of water to the boil and add the lemon juice and fennel. Cook for 2–3 minutes to blanch, drain and place in a greased ovenproof dish.

2 Beat the soft cheese in a bowl until smooth. Add the cream, milk and beaten egg, and whisk together until combined. Season with salt and pepper and pour the mixture over the fennel.

3 Melt 15 g/½ oz/1 tbsp of the butter in a small frying pan (skillet) and fry the caraway seeds gently for 1–2 minutes, until they release their aroma. Sprinkle them over the fennel.

4 Melt the remaining butter in a frying pan (skillet). Add the breadcrumbs and fry over a low heat, stirring frequently, until lightly browned. Sprinkle them evenly over the surface of the fennel.

5 Place in a preheated oven, 180°C/350°F/Gas Mark 4, and bake for 25–30 minutes, or until the fennel is tender. Serve immediately, garnished with sprigs of parsley.

Vegetable Cake

This is a savoury version of a cheesecake with a layer of fried potatoes as a delicious base. Use frozen mixed vegetables for the topping, if liked.

NUTRITIONAL INFORMATION

Calories	502	Sugars	8g
Protein	16g	Fat	31g
Carbohydrate	41g	Saturates	14g

20 MINS

45 MINS

SERVES 4

INGREDIENTS

BASE

- 2 tbsp vegetable oil, plus extra for brushing
- 4 large waxy potatoes, thinly sliced

TOPPING

- 1 tbsp vegetable oil
- 1 leek, chopped
- 1 courgette (zucchini), grated
- 1 red (bell) pepper, seeded and diced
- 1 green (bell) pepper, seeded and diced
- 1 carrot, grated
- 2 tsp chopped parsley
- 225 g/8 oz/1 cup full-fat soft cheese
- 25 g/1 oz/¼ cup grated mature (sharp) cheese
- 2 eggs, beaten
- salt and pepper
- shredded cooked leek, to garnish
- salad, to serve

2

4

5

1 Brush a 20 cm/8 inch springform cake tin (pan) with oil.

2 To make the base, heat the oil in a frying pan (skillet). Cook the potato slices until softened and browned. Drain on kitchen paper (paper towels) and place in the base of the tin (pan).

3 To make the topping, heat the oil in a separate frying pan (skillet). Add the leek and fry over a low heat, stirring frequently, for 3-4 minutes, until softened.

4 Add the courgette (zucchini), (bell) peppers, carrot and parsley to the pan and cook over a low heat for 5-7 minutes, or until the vegetables have softened.

5 Meanwhile, beat the cheeses and eggs together in a bowl. Stir in the vegetables and season to taste with salt and pepper. Spoon the mixture evenly over the potato base.

6 Cook in a preheated oven, 190°C/375°F/Gas Mark 5, for 20–25 minutes, until the cake is set.

7 Remove the vegetable cake from the tin (pan), transfer to a warm serving plate, garnish with shredded leek and serve with a crisp salad.

Vegetable Hot Pot

In this recipe, a variety of vegetables are cooked under a layer of potatoes, topped with cheese and cooked until golden brown.

NUTRITIONAL INFORMATION

Calories	279	Sugars	12g
Protein	10g	Fat	11g
Carbohydrate	34g	Saturates	4g

25 MINS

1 HOUR

SERVES 4

INGREDIENTS

- 2 large potatoes, thinly sliced
- 2 tbsp vegetable oil
- 1 red onion, halved and sliced
- 1 leek, sliced
- 2 garlic cloves, crushed
- 1 carrot, cut into chunks
- 100 g/3½ oz broccoli florets
- 100 g/3½ oz cauliflower florets
- 2 small turnips, quartered
- 1 tbsp plain (all-purpose) flour
- 700 ml/1¼ pints/3 cups vegetable stock
- 150 ml/¼ pint/⅔ cup dry cider
- 1 eating apple, cored and sliced
- 2 tbsp chopped sage
- pinch of cayenne pepper
- 50 g/1¾ oz/½ cup grated Cheddar cheese
- salt and pepper

1 Cook the potato slices in a saucepan of boiling water for 10 minutes. Drain thoroughly and reserve.

2 Heat the oil in a flameproof casserole. Add the onion, leek and garlic and sauté, stirring occasionally, for 2–3 minutes. Add the remaining vegetables and cook, stirring constantly, for a further 3–4 minutes.

2

3 Stir in the flour and cook for 1 minute. Gradually add the stock and cider and bring to the boil. Add the apple, sage and cayenne pepper and season well. Remove from the heat and transfer the vegetables to an ovenproof dish.

3

4 Arrange the potato slices on top of the vegetable mixture to cover.

4

5 Sprinkle the cheese on top of the potato slices and cook in a preheated oven, 190°C/375°F/Gas Mark 5, for 30–35 minutes or until the potato is golden brown and beginning to crispen around the edges. Serve immediately.

Lentil Roast

The perfect dish to serve for Sunday lunch. Roast vegetables make a succulent accompaniment.

NUTRITIONAL INFORMATION

Calories	400	Sugars	2g
Protein	26g	Fat	20g
Carbohydrate	32g	Saturates	10g

15 MINS — 1 HR 20 MINS

SERVES 6

INGREDIENTS

- 225 g/8 oz/1 cup red lentils
- 450 ml/16 fl oz/2 cups vegetable stock
- 1 bay leaf
- 15 g/½ oz/1 tbsp butter or margarine, softened
- 2 tbsp dried wholemeal (whole wheat) breadcrumbs
- 225 g/8 oz/2 cups grated mature (sharp) Cheddar cheese
- 1 leek, finely chopped
- 125 g/4½ oz button mushrooms, finely chopped
- 90 g/3 oz/1½ cups fresh wholemeal (whole wheat) breadcrumbs
- 2 tbsp chopped parsley
- 1 tbsp lemon juice
- 2 eggs, lightly beaten
- salt and pepper
- flat leaf parsley sprigs, to garnish
- mixed roast vegetables, to serve

1 Put the lentils, stock and bay leaf in a saucepan. Bring to the boil, cover and simmer gently for 15–20 minutes, until all the liquid is absorbed and the lentils have softened. Discard the bay leaf.

2 Base-line a 1 kg/2 lb 4 oz loaf tin (pan) with baking parchment. Grease with the butter or margarine and sprinkle with the dried breadcrumbs.

3 Stir the cheese, leek, mushrooms, fresh breadcrumbs and parsley into the lentils.

4 Bind the mixture together with the lemon juice and eggs. Season with salt and pepper. Spoon into the prepared loaf tin (pan) and smooth the top.

5 Bake in a preheated oven, 190°C/375°F/Gas Mark 5, for about 1 hour, until golden.

6 Loosen the loaf with a palette knife (spatula) and turn on to a warmed serving plate. Garnish with parsley and serve sliced, with roast vegetables.

2

3

4

Winter Vegetable Casserole

This hearty supper dish is best served with plenty of warm crusty bread to mop up the delicious juices.

NUTRITIONAL INFORMATION

Calories	211	Sugars	6g
Protein	11g	Fat	6g
Carbohydrate	26g	Saturates	0.8g

10 MINS 40 MINS

SERVES 4

INGREDIENTS

- 1 tbsp olive oil
- 1 red onion, halved and sliced
- 3 garlic cloves, crushed
- 225 g/8 oz spinach
- 1 fennel bulb, cut into eight
- 1 red (bell) pepper, seeded and cubed
- 1 tbsp plain (all-purpose) flour
- 450 ml/16 fl oz/1¾ cups vegetable stock
- 6 tbsp dry white wine
- 400 g/14 oz can chickpeas (garbanzo beans), drained
- 1 bay leaf
- 1 tsp ground coriander
- ½ tsp paprika
- salt and pepper
- fennel fronds, to garnish

1

2

4

1 Heat the olive oil in a large flameproof casserole. Add the onion and garlic and sauté over a low heat, stirring frequently, for 1 minute. Add the spinach and cook, stirring occasionally, for 4 minutes, or until wilted.

2 Add the fennel pieces and red (bell) pepper and cook, stirring constantly, for 2 minutes.

3 Stir in the flour and cook, stirring constantly, for 1 minute.

4 Add the vegetable stock, white wine, chickpeas (garbanzo beans), bay leaf, ground coriander and paprika, cover and simmer for 30 minutes. Season to taste with salt and pepper, garnish with fennel fronds and serve immediately straight from the casserole.

COOK'S TIP

Use other canned pulses or mixed beans instead of the chickpeas (garbanzo beans), if you prefer.

Cauliflower Bake

The red of the tomatoes is a great contrast to the cauliflower and herbs, making this dish appealing to both the eye and the palate.

NUTRITIONAL INFORMATION	
Calories 305	Sugars 9g
Protein 15g	Fat 14g
Carbohydrate ...31g	Saturates 6g

10 MINS — 40 MINS

SERVES 4

INGREDIENTS

- 500 g/1 lb 2 oz cauliflower, broken into florets
- 2 large potatoes, cubed
- 100 g/3½ oz cherry tomatoes

SAUCE

- 25 g/1 oz/2 tbsp butter or margarine
- 1 leek, sliced
- 1 garlic clove, crushed
- 25 g/1 oz/3 tbsp plain (all-purpose) flour
- 300 ml/½ pint/1¼ cups milk
- 75 g/2¾ oz/¾ cup mixed grated cheese, such as Cheddar, Parmesan and Gruyère (Swiss)
- ½ tsp paprika
- 2 tbsp chopped flat leaf parsley
- salt and pepper
- chopped parsley, to garnish

1 Cook the cauliflower in a saucepan of boiling water for 10 minutes. Drain well and reserve. Meanwhile, cook the potatoes in a pan of boiling water for 10 minutes, drain and reserve.

2 To make the sauce, melt the butter or margarine in a saucepan and sauté the leek and garlic for 1 minute. Stir in the flour and cook, stirring constantly, for 1 minute. Remove the pan from the heat and gradually stir in the milk, 50 g/1¾ oz/½ cup of the cheese, the paprika and parsley. Return the pan to the heat and bring to the boil, stirring constantly. Season with salt and pepper to taste.

3 Spoon the cauliflower into a deep ovenproof dish. Add the cherry tomatoes and top with the potatoes. Pour the sauce over the potatoes and sprinkle on the remaining cheese.

4 Cook in a preheated oven, 180°C/350°F/Gas Mark 4, for 20 minutes, or until the vegetables are cooked through and the cheese is golden brown and bubbling. Garnish and serve immediately.

2

3

3

VARIATION

This dish could be made with broccoli instead of the cauliflower as an alternative.

Lentil & Rice Casserole

This is a really hearty dish, perfect for cold days when a filling hot dish is just what you need.

NUTRITIONAL INFORMATION			
Calories	312	Sugars	9g
Protein	20g	Fat	2g
Carbohydrate	51g	Saturates	0.4g

15 MINS 40 MINS

SERVES 4

INGREDIENTS

225 g/8 oz/1 cup split red lentils
50 g/1¾ oz/⅓ cup long grain white rice
1.2 litres/2 pints/5 cups vegetable stock
1 leek, cut into chunks
3 garlic cloves, crushed
400 g/14 oz can chopped tomatoes
1 tsp ground cumin
1 tsp chilli powder
1 tsp garam masala
1 red (bell) pepper, seeded and sliced
100 g/3½ oz small broccoli florets
8 baby corn cobs, halved lengthways
50 g/1¾ oz French (green) beans, halved
1 tbsp shredded basil
salt and pepper
fresh basil sprigs, to garnish

1 Place the lentils, rice and vegetable stock in a large flameproof casserole and cook over a low heat, stirring occasionally, for 20 minutes.

2 Add the leek, garlic, tomatoes and their can juice, ground cumin, chilli powder, garam masala, sliced (bell) pepper, broccoli, corn cobs and French (green) beans to the pan .

3 Bring the mixture to the boil, reduce the heat, cover and simmer for a further 10–15 minutes, or until the vegetables are tender.

4 Add the shredded basil and season with salt and pepper to taste.

5 Garnish with fresh basil sprigs and serve immediately.

VARIATION

You can vary the rice in this recipe – use brown or wild rice, if you prefer.

Mushroom & Nut Crumble

A filling, tasty dish that is ideal for a warming family supper. The crunchy topping is flavoured with three different types of nuts.

NUTRITIONAL INFORMATION

Calories	779	Sugars	5g
Protein	16g	Fat	59g
Carbohydrate	48g	Saturates	14g

20 MINS 55 MINS

SERVES 4

INGREDIENTS

- 350 g/12 oz/5 cups sliced open-cup mushrooms
- 350 g/12 oz/5 cups sliced chestnut (crimini) mushrooms
- 400 ml/14 fl oz/1¾ cups vegetable stock
- 60 g/2 oz/¼ cup butter or margarine
- 1 large onion, finely chopped
- 1 garlic clove, crushed
- 60 g/2 oz/½ cup plain (all-purpose) flour
- 4 tbsp double (heavy) cream
- 2 tbsp chopped parsley
- salt and pepper
- herbs, to garnish

CRUMBLE TOPPING

- 90 g/3 oz/¾ cup medium oatmeal
- 90 g/3 oz/¾ cup wholemeal (whole wheat) flour
- 25 g/1 oz/¼ cup ground almonds
- 25 g/1 oz/¼ cup finely chopped walnuts
- 60 g/2 oz/½ cup finely chopped unsalted shelled pistachio nuts
- 1 tsp dried thyme
- 90 g/3 oz/⅓ cup butter or margarine, softened
- 1 tbsp fennel seeds

1 Put the mushrooms and stock in a large saucepan, bring to the boil, cover and simmer for 15 minutes, until tender. Drain, reserving the stock.

2 In another saucepan, melt the butter or margarine and fry the onion and garlic for 2–3 minutes, until just soft. Stir in the flour and cook for 1 minute.

3 Remove from the heat and gradually stir in the reserved mushroom stock. Return to the heat and cook, stirring, until thickened. Stir in the mushrooms, seasoning, cream and parsley and spoon into a shallow ovenproof dish.

4 To make the topping, in a bowl, mix together the oatmeal, flour, nuts, thyme and plenty of salt and pepper to taste.

5 Using a fork, mix in the butter or margarine until the topping resembles coarse breadcrumbs.

6 Sprinkle the topping mixture evenly over the mushrooms and then sprinkle with the fennel seeds. Bake in a preheated oven, at 190°C/375°F/Gas Mark 5, for about 25–30 minutes, or until the topping is golden and crisp. Garnish with fresh herbs and serve immediately.

1

3

6

Vine (Grape) Leaf Parcels

A wonderful combination of soft cheese, chopped dates, ground almonds and lightly fried nuts is encased in vine (grape) leaves.

NUTRITIONAL INFORMATION

Calories	459	Sugars	8g
Protein	12g	Fat	42g
Carbohydrate	9g	Saturates	20g

25 MINS 15 MINS

SERVES 4

INGREDIENTS

- 300 g/10½ oz/1¼ cups full-fat soft cheese
- 60 g/2 oz/¼ cup ground almonds
- 25 g/1 oz/2 tbsp dates, pitted and chopped
- 25 g/1 oz/2 tbsp butter
- 25 g/1 oz/¼ cup flaked (slivered) almonds
- 12–16 vine (grape) leaves
- salt and pepper
- barbecued (grilled) baby corn, to serve

TO GARNISH

- rosemary sprigs
- tomato wedges

1 Beat the soft cheese in a large bowl until smooth. Add the ground almonds and chopped dates, and mix together thoroughly. Season to taste with salt and pepper.

2 Melt the butter in a small frying pan (skillet). Add the flaked (slivered) almonds and fry over a very low heat, stirring constantly, for 2–3 minutes, until golden brown. Remove from the heat and set aside to cool for a few minutes.

3 Mix the fried almonds into the soft cheese mixture, stirring well to combine thoroughly.

1

3

4

4 Soak the vine (grape) leaves in water to remove some of the saltiness, if specified on the packet. Drain them, lay them out on a work surface (counter) and spoon an equal amount of the soft cheese mixture on to each one. Fold over the leaves to enclose the filling.

5 Wrap the vine (grape) leaf parcels in foil, 1 or 2 per foil package. Place over the barbecue (grill) to heat through for about 8–10 minutes, turning once. Serve with barbecued (grilled) baby corn and garnish with sprigs of rosemary and tomato wedges.

Tofu (Bean Curd) Skewers

Tofu (bean curd) is full of protein, vitamins and minerals and it develops a fabulous flavour when it is marinated in garlic and herbs.

NUTRITIONAL INFORMATION

Calories	149	Sugars	5g
Protein	13g	Fat	9g
Carbohydrate	5g	Saturates	1g

45 MINS · 15 MINS

SERVES 4

INGREDIENTS

- 350 g/12 oz tofu (bean curd)
- 1 red (bell) pepper
- 1 yellow (bell) pepper
- 2 courgettes (zucchini)
- 8 button mushrooms
- slices of lemon, to garnish

MARINADE

- grated rind and juice of ½ lemon
- 1 garlic clove, crushed
- ½ tsp rosemary, chopped
- ½ tsp chopped thyme
- 1 tbsp walnut oil

1 To make the marinade, combine the lemon rind and juice, garlic, rosemary, thyme and oil in a shallow dish.

2 Drain the tofu (bean curd), pat it dry on kitchen paper (paper towels) and cut it into squares with a sharp knife. Add to the marinade and toss to coat thoroughly. Set aside to marinate for 20–30 minutes.

3 Meanwhile, seed the (bell) peppers and cut the flesh into 2.5 cm/1 inch pieces. Blanch in a saucepan of boiling water for 4 minutes, refresh in cold water and drain.

2

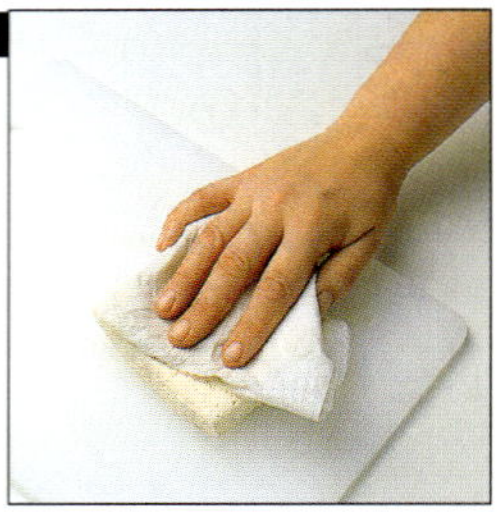

3

4

4 Using a canelle knife or swivel vegetable peeler, remove strips of peel from the courgettes (zucchini). Cut the courgettes (zucchini) into 2.5 cm/ 1 inch chunks.

5 Remove the tofu (bean curd) from the marinade, reserving the marinade for basting. Thread the tofu (bean curd) on to 8 skewers, alternating with the (bell) peppers, courgette (zucchini) and button mushrooms.

6 Barbecue (grill) the skewers over medium hot coals for about 6 minutes, turning and basting with the marinade.

7 Transfer the skewers to serving plates, garnish with lemon slices and serve.

Tasty Barbecue Sauce

Just the thing for brushing on to vegetable kebabs (kabobs) and burgers, this sauce is easy and quick to make.

NUTRITIONAL INFORMATION

Calories	100	Sugars	9g
Protein	1g	Fat	6g
Carbohydrate	10g	Saturates	1g

5 MINS 40 MINS

SERVES 4

INGREDIENTS

- 25 g/1 oz/2 tbsp butter or margarine
- 1 garlic clove, crushed
- 1 onion, finely chopped
- 400 g/14 oz can chopped tomatoes
- 1 tbsp dark muscovado sugar
- 1 tsp hot chilli sauce
- 1–2 gherkins
- 1 tbsp capers, drained
- salt and pepper

1 Melt the butter or margarine in a saucepan and fry the garlic and onion for 8–10 minutes, until well browned.

2 Add the chopped tomatoes, sugar and chilli sauce. Bring to the boil, then reduce the heat and simmer gently for 20–25 minutes, until thick and pulpy.

COOK'S TIP

To make sure that the sauce has a good colour, it is important to brown the onions really well to begin with. When fresh tomatoes are cheap and plentiful, they can be used instead of canned ones. Peel and chop 500 g/1 lb 2 oz.

2

3

3

3 Chop the gherkins and capers finely. Add to the sauce, stirring to mix. Cook the sauce over a low heat for 2 minutes.

4 Taste the sauce and season with a little salt and pepper to taste. Use as a baste for vegetarian kebabs (kabobs) and burgers, or as an accompaniment to other barbecued (grilled) food.

Pumpkin Parcels with Chilli

This spicy side dish is perfect for a Hallowe'en or Bonfire Night barbecue (grill) party, although it is equally delicious on a summer evening, too.

NUTRITIONAL INFORMATION

Energy	118	Sugar	3g
Protein	1g	Fat	11g
Carbohydrates	4g	Saturates	4g

10 MINS

25–30 MINS

SERVES 4

INGREDIENTS

700 g/1 lb 9 oz pumpkin or squash

2 tbsp sunflower oil

25 g/1 oz/2 tbsp butter

½ tsp chilli sauce

grated rind of 1 lime

2 tsp lime juice

1 Halve the pumpkin or squash and scoop out the seeds. Rinse the seeds and reserve. Cut the pumpkin into thin wedges and peel.

2 Heat the oil and butter together in a large saucepan, stirring constantly, until melted. Stir in the chilli sauce, lime rind and juice.

3 Add the pumpkin or squash and seeds to the pan and toss to coat all over in the flavoured butter.

4 Divide the mixture between 4 double thickness sheets of kitchen foil. Fold over the kitchen foil to enclose the pumpkin or squash mixture completely.

5 Barbecue (grill) the foil parcels over hot coals for 15–25 minutes, or until the pumpkin or squash is tender.

2

3

4

6 Transfer the foil parcels to warm serving plates. Open the parcels at the table and serve at once.

VARIATION

Add 2 teaspoons of curry paste to the oil instead of the lime and chilli. Use butternut squash when pumpkin is not available.

Turkish Kebabs (Kabobs)

A spicy chickpea (garbanzo bean) sauce is served with barbecued (grilled) colourful vegetable kebabs (kabobs).

NUTRITIONAL INFORMATION

Calories	303	Sugars	13g
Protein	13g	Fat	15g
Carbohydrate	30g	Saturates	2g

20 MINS 20 MINS

SERVES 4

INGREDIENTS

SAUCE

- 4 tbsp olive oil
- 3 garlic cloves, crushed
- 1 small onion, finely chopped
- 425 g/15 oz can chickpeas (garbanzo beans), rinsed and drained
- 300 ml/½ pint/1¼ cups natural (unsweetened) yogurt
- 1 tsp ground cumin
- ½ tsp chilli powder
- lemon juice
- salt and pepper

KEBABS (KABOBS)

- 1 aubergine (eggplant)
- 1 red (bell) pepper, seeded
- 1 green (bell) pepper, seeded
- 4 plum tomatoes
- 1 lemon, cut into wedges
- 8 small fresh bay leaves
- olive oil, for brushing

1 To make the sauce, heat the olive oil in a small frying pan (skillet). Add the garlic and onion and fry over a medium heat, stirring occasionally, for about 5 minutes, until the onion is softened and golden brown.

2 Put the chickpeas (garbanzo beans) and yogurt into a blender or food processor and add the cumin, chilli powder and onion mixture. Process for about 15 seconds, until smooth. Alternatively, mash the chickpeas (garbanzo beans) with a potato masher and stir in the yogurt, ground cumin, chilli powder and onion.

3 Place the puréed mixture in a bowl and season to taste with lemon juice, salt and pepper. Cover and chill until ready to serve.

4 To prepare the kebabs (kabobs), cut the vegetables into large chunks and thread them on to 4 skewers, placing a bay leaf and lemon wedge at both ends of each kebab (kabob).

5 Brush the kebabs (kabobs) with olive oil and cook them over the barbecue (grill), turning frequently, for 5–8 minutes. Heat the chickpea (garbanzo bean) sauce and serve with the kebabs (kabobs).

2

3

4

Citrus & Herb Marinades

Choose one of these marinades to give a marvellous flavour to barbecued food. The nutritional information is for Orange & Marjoram only.

NUTRITIONAL INFORMATION			
Calories	269	Sugars	3g
Protein	0.4g	Fat	6g
Carbohydrate	3g	Saturates	1g

20 MINS 0 MINS

SERVES 4

INGREDIENTS

ORANGE & MARJORAM

- 1 orange
- 125 ml/4 fl oz/½ cup olive oil
- 4 tbsp dry white wine
- 4 tbsp white wine vinegar
- 1 tbsp snipped chives
- 1 tbsp chopped marjoram
- salt and pepper

THAI-SPICED LIME

- 1 lemon grass stalk
- finely grated rind and juice of 1 lime
- 4 tbsp sesame oil
- 2 tbsp light soy sauce
- pinch of ground ginger
- 1 tbsp chopped coriander (cilantro)
- salt and pepper

BASIL & LEMON

- finely grated rind of 1 lemon
- 4 tbsp lemon juice
- 1 tbsp balsamic vinegar
- 2 tbsp red wine vinegar
- 2 tbsp virgin olive oil
- 1 tbsp chopped oregano
- 1 tbsp chopped basil
- salt and pepper

1 To make the Orange & Marjoram marinade, remove the rind from the orange with a zester, or grate it finely, then squeeze the juice.

2 Mix the orange rind and juice with all the remaining ingredients in a small bowl, whisking together to combine. Season with salt and pepper.

3 To make the Thai-Spiced Lime marinade, bruise the lemon grass by crushing it with a rolling pin. Mix the remaining ingredients together in a small bowl and add the lemon grass.

4 To make the Basil & Lemon marinade, whisk all the ingredients together in a small bowl. Season to taste with salt and pepper.

5 Keep the marinades covered with clear film (plastic wrap) or store them in screw-top jars, ready for using as marinades or bastes.

2

3

4

Sidekick Vegetables

Colourful vegetables are barbecued (grilled) over hot coals to make this unusual hot salad, which is served with a spicy chilli sauce on the side.

NUTRITIONAL INFORMATION	
Calories 224	Sugars 14g
Protein 4g	Fat 15g
Carbohydrate ...21g	Saturates 2g

15 MINS

30 MINS

SERVES 4

INGREDIENTS

- 1 red (bell) pepper, seeded
- 1 orange or yellow (bell) pepper, seeded
- 2 courgettes (zucchini)
- 2 corn cobs
- 1 aubergine (eggplant)
- olive oil, for brushing
- chopped thyme, rosemary and parsley
- salt and pepper
- lime or lemon wedges, to serve

DRESSING

- 2 tbsp olive oil
- 1 tbsp sesame oil
- 1 garlic clove, crushed
- 1 small onion, finely chopped
- 1 celery stick, finely chopped
- 1 small green chilli, seeded and chopped
- 4 tomatoes, chopped
- 5 cm/2 inch piece of cucumber, chopped
- 1 tbsp tomato purée (paste)
- 1 tbsp lime or lemon juice

1

2

4

1 To make the dressing, heat the olive and sesame oils together in a saucepan or frying pan (skillet). Add the garlic and onion, and fry over a low heat for about 3 minutes, until softened.

2 Add the celery, chilli and tomatoes to the pan and cook, stirring frequently, for 5 minutes.

3 Stir in the cucumber, tomato purée (paste) and lime or lemon juice, and simmer over a low heat for 8–10 minutes, until thick and pulpy. Season to taste with salt and pepper.

4 Cut the vegetables into thick slices and brush with a little olive oil.

5 Cook the vegetables over the hot coals of the barbecue (grill) for about 5–8 minutes, sprinkling them with salt and pepper and fresh herbs as they cook, and turning once.

6 Divide the vegetables between 4 serving plates and spoon some of the dressing on to the side. Serve at once, sprinkled with a few more chopped herbs and accompanied by the lime or lemon wedges.

Barbecued (Grilled) Bean Pot

Cook this tasty vegetable and Quorn (myco-protein) casserole conventionally, then keep it piping hot over the barbecue (grill).

NUTRITIONAL INFORMATION

Calories	381	Sugars	17g
Protein	21g	Fat	19g
Carbohydrate	34g	Saturates	3g

10 MINS — 1 HOUR

SERVES 4

INGREDIENTS

- 60 g/2 oz/¼ cup butter or margarine
- 1 large onion, chopped
- 2 garlic cloves, crushed
- 2 carrots, sliced
- 2 celery sticks, sliced
- 1 tbsp paprika
- 2 tsp ground cumin
- 400 g/14 oz can of chopped tomatoes
- 425 g/15 oz can of mixed beans, rinsed and drained
- 150 ml/¼ pint/⅔ cup vegetable stock
- 1 tbsp molasses sugar or black treacle (molasses)
- 350 g/12 oz Quorn (myco-protein) or soya cubes
- salt and pepper
- crusty French bread, to serve

1 Melt the butter or margarine in a large flameproof casserole and fry the onion and garlic over a medium heat, stirring occasionally, for about 5 minutes, until golden brown.

2 Add the carrots and celery and cook, stirring occasionally, for a further 2 minutes, then stir in the paprika and ground cumin.

3 Add the tomatoes and beans. Pour in the stock and add the sugar or treacle (molasses). Bring to the boil, then reduce the heat and simmer, uncovered, stirring occasionally, for 30 minutes.

4 Add the Quorn (myco-protein) or soya cubes to the casserole, cover and cook, stirring occasionally, for a further 20 minutes.

5 Season to taste, then transfer the casserole to the barbecue (grill), setting it to one side to keep hot.

6 Ladle on to plates and serve with crusty French bread.

1

3

4

VARIATION

If you prefer, cook the casserole in a preheated oven, 190°C/375°F/Gas Mark 5 from step 3, but keep the dish covered. Instead of mixed beans you could use just one type of canned beans.

Hot Salad

This quickly-made dish is ideal for a cold winter's night. Serve with crusty bread, freshly made rolls or garlic bread.

NUTRITIONAL INFORMATION

Calories	154	Sugars	13g
Protein	4g	Fat	9g
Carbohydrate	14g	Saturates	6g

10 MINS | 10 MINS

SERVES 4

INGREDIENTS

- ½ medium-sized cauliflower
- 1 green (bell) pepper
- 1 red (bell) pepper
- ½ cucumber
- 4 carrots
- 2 tbsp butter
- salt and pepper
- crusty bread, rolls or garlic bread, to serve

DRESSING

- 3 tbsp olive oil
- 1 tbsp white wine vinegar
- 1 tbsp light soy sauce
- 1 tsp caster (superfine) sugar
- salt and pepper

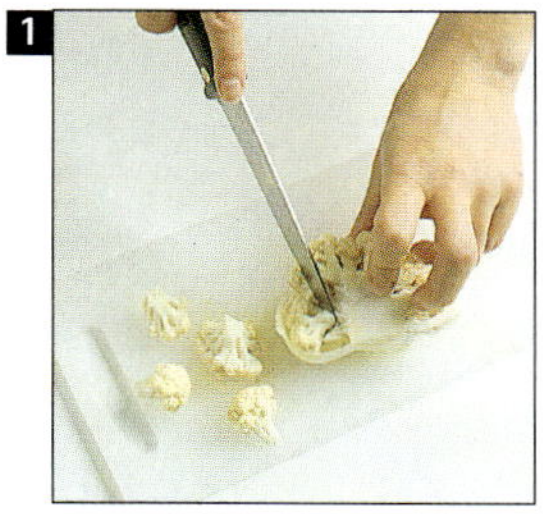

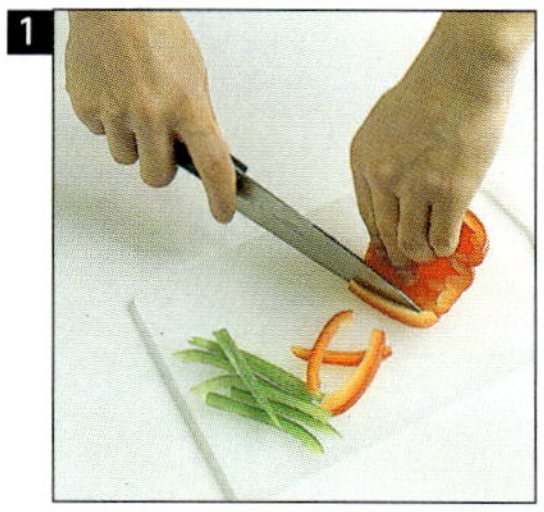

1 Cut the cauliflower into small florets, using a sharp knife. Seed the (bell) peppers and cut the flesh into thin slices. Cut the cucumber into thin slices. Thinly slice the carrots lengthways.

2 Melt the butter in a large heavy-based saucepan. Add the cauliflower florets, (bell) peppers, cucumber and carrots and fry over a medium heat, stirring constantly, for 5-7 minutes, until tender, but still firm to the bite. Season with salt and pepper. Lower the heat, cover with a lid, and simmer for 3 minutes.

3 Meanwhile, make the dressing. Whisk together all the ingredients until thoroughly combined.

4 Transfer the vegetables to a serving dish, pour over the dressing, toss to mix well and serve immediately.

VARIATION

You can replace the vegetables in this recipe with those of your choice, such as broccoli, spring onions (scallions) and courgettes (zucchini).

Mexican Salad

This is a colourful salad with a Mexican theme, using beans, tomatoes and avocado. The chilli dressing adds a little kick.

NUTRITIONAL INFORMATION

Calories	307	Sugars	7g
Protein	5g	Fat	26g
Carbohydrate	13g	Saturates	5g

10–15 MINS 0 MINS

SERVES 4

INGREDIENTS

- lollo rosso lettuce
- 2 ripe avocados
- 2 tsp lemon juice
- 4 medium tomatoes
- 1 onion
- 175 g/6 oz/2 cups mixed canned beans, drained

DRESSING

- 4 tbsp olive oil
- drop of chilli oil
- 2 tbsp garlic wine vinegar
- pinch of caster (superfine) sugar
- pinch of chilli powder
- 1 tbsp chopped parsley

1

3

4

1 Line a large serving bowl with the lettuce leaves.

2 Using a sharp knife, cut the avocados in half and remove the stones (pits). Thinly slice the flesh and sprinkle with the lemon juice.

3 Thinly slice the tomatoes and onion and push the onion out into rings. Arrange the avocado, tomatoes and onion around the salad bowl, leaving a space in the centre.

4 Spoon the beans into the centre of the salad and whisk the dressing ingredients together. Pour the dressing over the salad and serve.

COOK'S TIP

The lemon juice is sprinkled on to the avocados to prevent discoloration when in contact with the air. For this reason the salad should be prepared, assembled and served quite quickly.

Gado Gado

This is a well-known and very popular Indonesian salad of mixed vegetables with a peanut dressing.

NUTRITIONAL INFORMATION	
Calories 392	Sugars 8g
Protein 9g	Fat 35g
Carbohydrate 11g	Saturates 5g

10 MINS

25 MINS

SERVES 4

INGREDIENTS

- 100 g/3½ oz/1 cup shredded white cabbage
- 100 g/3½ oz French (green) beans, cut into three
- 100 g/3½ oz carrots, cut into matchsticks
- 100 g/3½ oz cauliflower florets
- 100 g/3½ oz beansprouts

DRESSING

- 100 ml/3½ fl oz/½ cup vegetable oil
- 100 g/3½ oz/1 cup unsalted peanuts
- 2 garlic cloves, crushed
- 1 small onion, finely chopped
- ½ tsp chilli powder
- ½ tsp light brown sugar
- 425 ml/¾ pint/2 cups water
- juice of ½ lemon
- salt
- sliced spring onions (scallions), to garnish

3

5

6

1 Cook the vegetables separately in a saucepan of salted boiling water for 4–5 minutes, drain well and chill.

2 To make the dressing, heat the oil in a frying pan (skillet) and fry the peanuts, tossing frequently, for 3–4 minutes.

3 Remove from the pan with a slotted spoon and drain on absorbent kitchen paper (paper towels). Process the peanuts in a food processor or crush with a rolling pin until a fine mixture is formed.

4 Pour all but 1 tablespoon of the oil from the pan and fry the garlic and onion for 1 minute. Add the chilli powder, sugar, a pinch of salt and the water and bring to the boil.

5 Stir in the peanuts. Reduce the heat and simmer for 4–5 minutes until the sauce thickens. Add the lemon juice and set aside to cool.

6 Arrange the vegetables in a serving dish and spoon the peanut dressing into the centre. Garnish and serve.

Alfalfa & Spinach Salad

This is a really refreshing salad that must be assembled just before serving to prevent everything being coloured by the beetroot (beet).

NUTRITIONAL INFORMATION

Calories	139	Sugars	7g
Protein	2g	Fat	11g
Carbohydrate	8g	Saturates	2g

10 MINS   0 MINS

SERVES 4

INGREDIENTS

- 100 g/3½ oz baby spinach
- 75 g/2¾ oz/1⅓ cups alfalfa sprouts
- 2 celery sticks, sliced
- 4 cooked beetroot (beets), cut into eight

DRESSING

- 4 tbsp olive oil
- 4½ tsp garlic wine vinegar
- 1 garlic clove, crushed
- 2 tsp clear honey
- 1 tbsp chopped chives

1 Place the spinach and alfalfa sprouts in a large bowl and mix together.

2 Add the celery to the bowl and mix together well.

3 Toss in the beetroot (beet) and mix until well combined.

4 To make the dressing, mix the oil, wine vinegar, garlic, honey and chopped chives.

5 Pour the dressing over the salad, toss well and serve immediately.

1

2

4

VARIATION

Add the segments of 1 large orange to the salad to make it even more colourful and refreshing. Replace the garlic wine vinegar with a different flavoured oil such as chilli or herb, if you prefer.

Moroccan Salad

Couscous is a type of semolina made from durum wheat. It is wonderful in salads, as it readily takes up the flavour of the dressing.

1

2

4

NUTRITIONAL INFORMATION

Calories	195	Sugars	15g
Protein	8g	Fat	2g
Carbohydrate	40g	Saturates	0.3g

30–35 MINS 0 MINS

SERVES 6

INGREDIENTS

- 175 g/6 oz/2 cups couscous
- 1 bunch spring onions (scallions), finely chopped
- 1 small green (bell) pepper, seeded and chopped
- 10 cm/4 inch piece of cucumber, chopped
- 175 g/6 oz can chickpeas (garbanzo beans), rinsed and drained
- 60 g/2 oz/⅔ cup sultanas (golden raisins) or raisins
- 2 oranges
- salt and pepper
- mint sprigs, to garnish
- lettuce leaves, to serve

DRESSING

- finely grated rind of 1 orange
- 1 tbsp chopped fresh mint
- 150 ml/¼ pint/⅔ cup natural yogurt

1 Put the couscous into a bowl and cover with boiling water. Leave it to soak for about 15 minutes to swell the grains, then stir gently with a fork to separate them.

2 Add the spring onions (scallions), green (bell) pepper, cucumber, chickpeas (garbanzo beans) and sultanas (golden raisins) or raisins to the couscous, stirring to combine. Season well with salt and pepper.

3 To make the dressing, place the orange rind, mint and yogurt in a bowl and mix together until well combined. Pour over the couscous mixture and stir to mix well.

4 Using a sharp serrated knife, remove the peel and pith from the oranges. Cut the flesh into segments, removing all the membrane.

5 Arrange the lettuce leaves on 4 serving plates. Divide the couscous mixture between the plates and arrange the orange segments on top. Garnish with sprigs of fresh mint and serve.

You could also use a ewe's milk cheese, such as feta, in this recipe for a sharper flavour.

Marinated Vegetable Salad

Multicoloured Salad

The beetroot (beet) adds a rich colour to this dish, tinting the potato an appealing pink. Mixed with cucumber it is a really vibrant salad.

NUTRITIONAL INFORMATION

Calories	174	Sugars	8g
Protein	4g	Fat	6g
Carbohydrate	27g	Saturates	1g

15-20 MINS — 20 MINS

SERVES 4

INGREDIENTS

- 500 g/1 lb 2 oz waxy potatoes, diced
- 4 small cooked beetroot (beets), sliced
- ½ small cucumber, thinly sliced
- 2 large dill pickles, sliced
- 1 red onion, halved and sliced
- dill sprigs, to garnish

DRESSING

- 1 garlic clove, crushed
- 2 tbsp olive oil
- 2 tbsp red wine vinegar
- 2 tbsp chopped fresh dill
- salt and pepper

1 Cook the diced potatoes in a saucepan of boiling water for about 15 minutes, or until just tender. Drain and set aside to cool.

2 When cool, mix the potato and beetroot (beets) together in a bowl and set aside.

3 To make the dressing, whisk together the garlic, olive oil, vinegar and dill and season to taste with salt and pepper.

4 When ready to serve, line a large serving platter with the slices of cucumber, dill pickles and red onion. Spoon the potato and beetroot (beet) mixture into the centre of the platter.

5 Pour the dressing over the salad and serve immediately, garnished with fresh dill sprigs.

2

4

5

VARIATION

Line the salad platter with 2 heads of chicory (endive), separated into leaves, and arrange the cucumber, dill pickle and red onion slices on top of the leaves.

Middle Eastern Salad

This attractive-looking salad can be served with a couple of vegetable kebabs (kabobs) for a delicious light lunch or an informal supper.

NUTRITIONAL INFORMATION

Calories	163	Sugars	12g
Protein	8g	Fat	3g
Carbohydrate	27g	Saturates	0.4g

15 MINS   0 MINS

SERVES 4

INGREDIENTS

- 400 g/14 oz can chickpeas (garbanzo beans)
- 4 carrots
- 1 bunch spring onions (scallions)
- 1 medium cucumber
- ½ tsp salt
- ½ tsp pepper
- 3 tbsp lemon juice
- 1 red (bell) pepper, sliced

1 Drain the chickpeas (garbanzo beans) and place them in a large salad bowl.

2 Using a sharp knife, thinly slice the carrots. Cut the spring onions (scallions) into small pieces. Thickly slice the cucumber and then cut the slices into quarters.

2 2 2

3 Add the carrot slices, spring onions (scallions) and cucumber to the chickpeas (garbanzo beans) and mix.

4 Season to taste with the salt and pepper and sprinkle with the lemon juice. Toss the salad ingredients together gently, using 2 serving spoons.

5 Using a sharp knife, thinly slice the red (bell) pepper. Arrange the slices of red (bell) pepper decoratively on top of the chickpea (garbanzo bean) salad. Serve the salad immediately or chill in the refrigerator and serve when required.

VARIATION

This salad would also be delicious made with ful medames. If they are not available canned, use 150g/5½ oz/1 cup dried, soaked for 5 hours and then simmered for 2½ hours. Another alternative would be canned gunga beans.

Kashmiri Spinach

This is an imaginative way to serve spinach, which adds a little zip to it. It is a very simple dish, which will complement almost any curry.

NUTRITIONAL INFORMATION

Calories	81	Sugars	2g
Protein	4g	Fat	7g
Carbohydrate	2g	Saturates	1g

5 MINS 25 MINS

SERVES 4

INGREDIENTS

- 500 g/1 lb 2 oz spinach or Swiss chard or baby leaf spinach
- 2 tbsp mustard oil
- ¼ tsp garam masala
- 1 tsp yellow mustard seeds
- 2 spring onions (scallions), sliced

1

3

5

1 Remove the tough stalks from the spinach.

2 Heat the mustard oil in a preheated wok or large heavy-based frying pan (skillet) until it smokes. Add the garam masala and mustard seeds. Cover the pan quickly – you will hear the mustard seeds popping inside.

3 When the popping has ceased, remove the cover, add the spring onions (scallions) and spinach. Cook, stirring constantly, until the spinach has wilted.

4 Continue cooking the spinach, uncovered, over a medium heat for 10–15 minutes, until most of the water has evaporated. If using frozen spinach, it will not need to cook for so long – cook it until most of the water has evaporated.

5 Remove the spinach and spring onions (scallions) with a slotted spoon, draining off any remaining liquid. (This dish is pleasanter to eat when it is served as dry as possible.)

6 Transfer to a warmed serving dish and serve immediately, while it is still piping hot.

COOK'S TIP

Mustard oil is made from mustard seeds and is very fiery when raw. However, when it is heated to this smoking stage, it loses a lot of the fire and takes on a delightful sweet quality.

Long Beans with Tomatoes

Indian meals often need some green vegetables to complement the spicy dishes and to set off the rich sauces.

NUTRITIONAL INFORMATION

Calories	76	Sugars	3g
Protein	2g	Fat	6g
Carbohydrate	4g	Saturates	3g

15 MINS 25 MINS

SERVES 6

INGREDIENTS

- 500 g/1 lb 2 oz green beans, cut into 5 cm/2 inch lengths
- 2 tbsp vegetable ghee
- 2.5 cm/1 inch piece of root ginger, grated
- 1 garlic clove, crushed
- 1 tsp turmeric
- ½ tsp cayenne
- 1 tsp ground coriander
- 4 tomatoes, peeled, seeded and diced
- 150 ml/¼ pint/⅔ cup vegetable stock

1 Blanch the beans briefly in boiling water, drain, refresh under cold running water and drain again.

2 Melt the ghee in a large saucepan over a moderate heat. Add the grated ginger and crushed garlic, stir and add the turmeric, cayenne and ground coriander. Stir over a low heat for about 1 minute, until fragrant.

3 Add the diced tomatoes, tossing them until they are thoroughly coated in the spice mix.

4 Add the vegetable stock to the pan, bring to the boil and cook over a medium-high heat, stirring occasionally, for about 10 minutes, until the sauce has thickened.

5 Add the beans, reduce the heat to moderate and heat through, stirring constantly, for 5 minutes.

6 Transfer to a warmed serving dish and serve immediately.

COOK'S TIP

Ginger graters are an invaluable piece of equipment to have when cooking Indian food. These small flat graters, made of either bamboo or china, can be held directly over the pan while you grate.

Broccoli with Fluffy Eggs

Broccoli or cauliflower florets in a mustard sauce are topped with an egg yolk set in whisked egg white and finished off with grated cheese.

NUTRITIONAL INFORMATION

Calories	733	Sugars	11g
Protein	43g	Fat	53g
Carbohydrate	23g	Saturates	25g

10 MINS 15 MINS

SERVES 1

INGREDIENTS

- 175 g/6 oz/1½ cups broccoli or cauliflower florets
- 15 g/½ oz/1 tbsp butter or margarine
- 15 g/½ oz/2 tbsp flour
- 150 ml/¼ pint/⅔ cup milk
- 1 tbsp coarse grain mustard
- dash of lemon juice
- 90 g/3 oz/¾ cup grated mature (sharp) Cheddar cheese
- 1 large egg, separated
- salt and pepper
- paprika, to garnish

1 Cook the broccoli or cauliflower in boiling lightly salted water for about 3–4 minutes, until tender, but still crisp.

2 Meanwhile, melt the butter or margarine in a small saucepan. Stir in the flour and cook, stirring constantly, for 1 minute. Gradually add the milk and bring to the boil, stirring constantly until thickened. Season to taste with salt and pepper. Stir in the mustard and lemon juice and simmer for 1–2 minutes.

3 Remove the sauce from the heat and stir in two-thirds of the grated cheese until melted.

4

5

6

4 Drain the broccoli or cauliflower very thoroughly and place on an ovenproof plate or dish. Pour the cheese sauce over the vegetables.

5 Whisk the egg white until very stiff and season lightly. Pile the egg white on top of the broccoli or cauliflower and make a well in the centre.

6 Drop the egg yolk into the well in the egg white and sprinkle with the remaining cheese. Place under a preheated moderate grill (broiler) for 3–4 minutes, until the meringue is lightly browned and the cheese has melted. Serve immediately, sprinkled with paprika.

Baby Cauliflowers

Whole baby cauliflowers coated with a red Leicester cheese and poppy seed sauce are cooked to perfection in the microwave oven.

NUTRITIONAL INFORMATION

Calories	173	Sugars	6g
Protein	8g	Fat	11g
Carbohydrate	10g	Saturates	6g

30 MINS 15 MINS

SERVES 4

INGREDIENTS

- 4 cloves
- ½ onion
- ½ carrot
- 1 bouquet garni
- 250 ml/9 fl oz/1 cup milk
- 4 baby cauliflowers
- 3 tbsp water
- 15 g/½ oz/1 tbsp butter
- 15 g/½ oz/2 tbsp plain (all-purpose) flour
- 60 g/2 oz/½ cup grated red Leicester cheese
- 1 tbsp poppy seeds
- pinch of paprika
- salt and pepper
- parsley to garnish

1 Stick the cloves into the onion. Place in a bowl with the carrot, bouquet garni and milk. Heat on HIGH power for 2½–3 minutes. Leave to stand for 20 minutes to allow the flavours to infuse.

2 Trim the base and leaves from the cauliflowers and scoop out the stem using a small sharp knife, leaving the cauliflowers intact. Place the cauliflowers upside down in a large dish. Add the water, cover and cook on HIGH power for 5 minutes, until just tender. Leave to stand for 2–3 minutes.

3 Put the butter in a bowl and cook on HIGH power for 30 seconds, until melted. Stir in the flour. Cook on HIGH power for 30 seconds.

4 Strain the milk into a jug, discarding the vegetables. Gradually add to the flour and butter, beating well between each addition. Cover and cook on HIGH power for 3 minutes, stirring every 30 seconds after the first minute, until the sauce has thickened.

5 Stir the cheese and poppy seeds into the sauce and season with salt and pepper to taste. Cover and cook on HIGH power for 30 seconds.

6 Drain the cauliflowers and arrange on a plate or in a shallow dish. Pour over the sauce and sprinkle with a little paprika. Cook on HIGH power for 1 minute to reheat. Serve garnished with fresh parsley.

1

2

6

Baked Celery with Cream

This dish is topped with breadcrumbs for a crunchy topping, underneath which is hidden a creamy celery and pecan mixture.

NUTRITIONAL INFORMATION	
Calories 237	Sugars 5g
Protein 7g	Fat 19g
Carbohydrate 11g	Saturates 7g

15 MINS   40 MINS

SERVES 4

INGREDIENTS

- 1 head of celery
- ½ tsp ground cumin
- ½ tsp ground coriander
- 1 garlic clove, crushed
- 1 red onion, thinly sliced
- 50 g/1¾ oz/½ cup pecan nut halves
- 150 ml/¼ pint/⅔ cup vegetable stock
- 150 ml/¼ pint/⅔ cup single (light) cream
- 50 g/1¾ oz/1 cup fresh wholemeal (whole wheat) breadcrumbs
- 25 g/1 oz/⅓ cup grated Parmesan cheese
- salt and pepper
- celery leaves, to garnish

1

2

3

COOK'S TIP

Once grated, Parmesan cheese quickly loses its 'bite' so it is best to grate only the amount you need for the recipe. Wrap the rest tightly in foil and it will keep for several months in the refrigerator.

1 Trim the celery and cut into matchsticks. Place the celery in an ovenproof dish, together with the ground cumin, coriander, garlic, red onion and pecan nuts.

2 Mix the stock and cream together and pour over the vegetables. Season with salt and pepper to taste.

3 Mix the breadcrumbs and cheese together and sprinkle over the top to cover the vegetables.

4 Cook in a preheated oven, 200°C/400°F/Gas Mark 6, for 40 minutes, or until the vegetables are tender and the top crispy. Garnish with celery leaves and serve at once.

Courgette (Zucchini) Curry

This delicious curry is spiced with fenugreek seeds, which have a beautiful aroma and a distinctive taste.

NUTRITIONAL INFORMATION			
Calories	188	Sugars	5g
Protein	3g	Fat	17g
Carbohydrate	6g	Saturates	2g

20 MINS

15 MINS

SERVES 4

INGREDIENTS

- 6 tbsp vegetable oil
- 1 medium onion, finely chopped
- 3 fresh green chillies, finely chopped
- 1 tsp finely chopped root ginger
- 1 tsp crushed garlic
- 1 tsp chilli powder
- 500 g/1 lb 2 oz courgettes (zucchini), thinly sliced
- 2 tomatoes, sliced
- fresh coriander (cilantro) leaves, plus extra to garnish
- 2 tsp fenugreek seeds
- chapatis, to serve

2

3

3

1 Heat the oil in a large, heavy-based frying pan (skillet).

2 Add the onion, fresh green chillies, ginger, garlic and chilli powder to the pan, stirring well to combine.

3 Add the sliced courgettes (zucchini) and the sliced tomatoes to the pan and stir-fry over a medium heat, for 5-7 minutes.

4 Add the cilantro (coriander) leaves and fenugreek seeds to the courgette (zucchini) mixture in the pan and stir-fry over a medium heat for 5 minutes, until the vegetables are tender.

5 Remove the pan from the heat and transfer the courgette (zucchini) and fenugreek seed mixture to serving dishes. Garnish and serve hot with chapatis.

VARIATION

You could use coriander seeds instead of the fenugreek seeds, if you prefer.

Easy Cauliflower & Broccoli

Whole baby cauliflowers are used in this recipe. Try to find them if you can, if not use large bunches of florets.

NUTRITIONAL INFORMATION			
Calories	433	Sugars	2g
Protein	8g	Fat	44g
Carbohydrate	3g	Saturates	9g

10 MINS 20 MINS

SERVES 4

INGREDIENTS

- 2 baby cauliflowers
- 225 g/8 oz broccoli
- salt and pepper

SAUCE

- 8 tbsp olive oil
- 4 tbsp butter or margarine
- 2 tsp grated root ginger
- juice and rind of 2 lemons
- 5 tbsp chopped coriander (cilantro)
- 5 tbsp grated Cheddar cheese

1 Using a sharp knife, cut the cauliflowers in half and the broccoli into very large florets.

2 Cook the cauliflower and broccoli in a saucepan of boiling salted water for 10 minutes. Drain well, transfer to a shallow ovenproof dish and keep warm until required.

3 To make the sauce, put the oil and butter or margarine in a pan and heat gently until the butter melts. Add the grated root ginger, lemon juice, lemon rind and coriander (cilantro) and simmer for 2–3 minutes, stirring occasionally.

4 Season the sauce with salt and pepper to taste, then pour over the vegetables in the dish and sprinkle the cheese on top.

5 Cook under a preheated hot grill (broiler) for 2–3 minutes, or until the cheese is bubbling and golden. Leave to cool for 1–2 minutes and then serve.

1

3

4

COOK'S TIP

Lime or orange could be used instead of the lemon for a fruity and refreshing sauce.

Chocolate Fudge Pudding

This pudding has a hidden surprise when cooked, as it separates to give a rich chocolate sauce at the bottom of the dish.

NUTRITIONAL INFORMATION			
Calories	397	Sugars	27g
Protein	10g	Fat	25g
Carbohydrate	36g	Saturates	5g

10 MINS — 40 MINS

SERVES 4

INGREDIENTS

- 50 g/1¾ oz/4 tbsp margarine, plus extra for greasing
- 75 g/2¾ oz/6 tbsp light brown sugar
- 2 eggs, beaten
- 350 ml/12 fl oz/1¼ cups milk
- 50 g/1¾ oz/½ cup chopped walnuts
- 40 g/1½ oz/¼ cup plain (all-purpose) flour
- 2 tbsp cocoa powder (unsweetened cocoa)
- icing (confectioners' sugar) and cocoa powder (unsweetened cocoa), to dust

1 Lightly grease a 1 litre/1¾ pint/4 cup ovenproof dish.

2 Cream together the margarine and sugar in a large mixing bowl until fluffy. Beat in the eggs.

3 Gradually stir in the milk and add the walnuts, stirring to mix.

4 Sift the flour and cocoa powder (unsweetened cocoa) into the mixture and fold in gently, with a metal spoon, until well mixed.

5 Spoon the mixture into the dish and cook in a preheated oven, 180°C/350°F/Gas Mark 4, for 35–40 minutes, or until the sponge is cooked.

6 Dust with sugar and cocoa powder (unsweetened cocoa) and serve.

VARIATION

Add 1–2 tbsp brandy or rum to the mixture for a slightly alcoholic pudding, or 1–2 tbsp orange juice for a child-friendly version.

Rice & Banana Brûlée

Take a can of rice pudding, flavour it with orange rind, stem (candied) ginger, raisins and sliced bananas and top with a brown sugar glaze.

NUTRITIONAL INFORMATION

Calories	509	Sugars	98g
Protein	9g	Fat	6g
Carbohydrate	112g	Saturates	4g

5 MINS 5 MINS

SERVES 2

INGREDIENTS

- 400 g/14 oz can creamed rice pudding
- grated rind of ½ orange
- 2 pieces stem (preserved) ginger, finely chopped
- 2 tsp ginger syrup from the jar
- 40 g/1½ oz/¼ cup raisins
- 1–2 bananas
- 1–2 tsp lemon juice
- 4–5 tbsp demerara (brown crystal) sugar

1 Empty the can of rice pudding into a bowl and mix in the grated orange rind, ginger, ginger syrup and raisins.

2 Cut the bananas diagonally into slices, toss in the lemon juice to prevent them from discolouring, drain and divide between 2 individual flameproof dishes.

3 Spoon the rice mixture in an even layer over the bananas so the dishes are almost full.

4 Sprinkle an even layer of sugar over the rice in each dish.

5 Place the dishes under a preheated moderate grill (broiler) and heat until the sugar melts, taking care the sugar does not burn.

6 Set aside to cool until the caramel sets, then chill in the refrigerator until ready to serve. Tap the caramel with the back of a spoon to break it.

COOK'S TIP

Canned rice pudding is very versatile and is delicious heated with orange segments and grated apples added. Try it served cold with grated chocolate and mixed chopped nuts stirred through it.

Tropical Fruit Fool

Fruit fools are always popular, and this light, tangy version will be no exception. Use your favourite fruits in this recipe if you prefer.

NUTRITIONAL INFORMATION			
Calories	149	Sugars	25g
Protein	6g	Fat	0.4g
Carbohydrate	32g	Saturates	0.2g

35 MINS   0 MINS

SERVES 4

INGREDIENTS

- 1 medium ripe mango
- 2 kiwi fruit
- 1 medium banana
- 2 tbsp lime juice
- ½ tsp finely grated lime rind, plus extra to decorate
- 2 medium egg whites
- 425 g/15 oz can low-fat custard
- ½ tsp vanilla essence (extract)
- 2 passion fruit

1 To peel the mango, slice either side of the smooth, flat central stone. Roughly chop the flesh and blend the fruit in a food processor or blender until smooth. Alternatively, mash with a fork.

1

2

4

2 Peel the kiwi fruit, chop the flesh into small pieces and place in a bowl. Peel and chop the banana and add to the bowl. Toss all of the fruit in the lime juice and rind and mix well.

3 In a grease-free bowl, whisk the egg whites until stiff and then gently fold in the custard and vanilla essence (extract) until thoroughly mixed.

4 In 4 tall glasses, alternately layer the chopped fruit, mango purée and custard mixture, finishing with the custard on top. Leave to chill in the refrigerator for 20 minutes.

5 Halve the passion fruits, scoop out the seeds and spoon the passion fruit over the fruit fools. Decorate each serving with the extra lime rind and serve.

VARIATION

Other tropical fruits to try include paw-paw (papaya) purée, with chopped pineapple and dates or pomegranate seeds to decorate. Or make a summer fruit fool by using strawberry purée, topped with raspberries and blackberries and cherries.

This is a Parragon Book
This edition published in 2003

Parragon
Queen Street House
4 Queen Street
Bath BA1 1HE, UK

ISBN: 1-40540-110-9

Printed in China

NOTE

This book uses metric and imperial measurements. Follow the same units of measurement throughout; do not mix metric and imperial. All spoon measurements are level: teaspoons are assumed to be 5 ml, and tablespoons are assumed to be 15 ml. Unless otherwise stated, milk is assumed to be full fat, eggs and individual vegetables such as potatoes are medium, and pepper is freshly ground black pepper.

The nutritional information provided for each recipe is per serving or per person. Optional ingredients variations or serving suggestions have not been included in the calculations. The times given for each recipe are an approximate guide only because the preparation times may differ according to the techniques used by different people and the cooking times may vary as a result of the type of oven used.

Recipes using raw or very lightly cooked eggs should be avoided by infants, the elderly, pregnant women, convalescents, and anyone suffering from an illness.

The publisher would like to thank Steamer Trading Cookshop, Lewes, East Sussex, for the kind loan of props.